# ENFORCEMENT

# OR

# NEGOTIATION

SUNY Series in Critical Issues in Criminal Justice
*Donald J. Newman, Gilbert Geis, and Terence P. Thornberry, Editors*

# ENFORCEMENT

# OR

# NEGOTIATION

*Constructing*
*A Regulatory*
*Bureaucracy*

NEAL SHOVER

DONALD A. CLELLAND

JOHN LYNXWILER

**State University of New York Press**

Published by
State University of New York Press, Albany

© 1986 State University of New York

All rights reserved

For information, address State University of New York
Press, State University Plaza, Albany, N.Y., 12246

**Library of Congress Cataloging in Publications Data**

Shover, Neal.
  Enforcement or negotiation.

  (SUNY series in critical issues in criminal justice)
  Bibliography: p.
  Includes index.
  1. Strip mining—Law and legislation—United States.
2. United States. Office of Surface Mining Reclamation
and Enforcement.  I. Clelland, Donald A. II.  Lynxwiler,
John.  III. Title.  IV. Series.
KF1823.S5  1986        353.0082'326        86-3695
ISBN 0-88706-343-8
ISBN 0-88706-342-X (pbk.)
  10  9  8  7  6  5  4  3  2  1

# Contents

Regulatory Reform
Inspection and Enforcement
State Responses
The Coal Industries
Environmentalists and Citizens' Groups
Conclusions

# Foreword

Strip mining—the surface mining of coal—is ugly. It is a productive process that scars the land and damages the surrounding environment. Because restoration is costly, the competitive pricing of coal discourages mining companies from engaging in adequate reclamation practices. Rapid growth of strip mining in the 1960s spurred political responses. State governments were compelled to become involved in the regulation of surface mining. However, states, too, are economic competitors and, thus, subject to a "Gresham's law of regulation" (Rowland and Marz, 1982)—bad regulation drives out good. In the context of broad social concern for the correction of environmental abuses, surface mining became a national issue. With the passage of the 1977 Surface Mining Control and Reclamation Act and the establishment of the Office of Surface Mining in the Department of the Interior, the federal government entered the arena. The mandate of the new regulatory agency was to control the environmental damages perpetrated by mining companies. The agency was to accomplish this goal by strengthening the authority and implementation practices of state regulators.

This book explores the early development and implementation of the federal program for regulation of surface mining (1977-1981). The manner in which regulatory bodies carry out their missions vary widely. Unlike most federal agencies, the Office of Surface Mining took a stringent stance on most aspects of its duties. Our analysis is guided by a typology that contrasts enforced compliance with negotiated compliance styles of regulation. We have attempted to explain how and why the new Office of Surface Mining developed rigorous enforced compliance policies and actions.

Regulation is a process. We examine the various stages of the regulatory process: the making of the law, the formation of the agency, the construction of regulations, and implementation in the field. The regulatory process is a political process at every stage. Our analysis takes account of the participants in the political arena: environmentalists, the coal industry, Congress, federal and state bureaucrats, state politicians, and the courts.

Regulation is also a calculated intrusion by the state into the workings of the economy. Recent years have been marked by a proliferation of neo-Marxist and non-Marxist theories of the state, yet few of these theories have addressed the problem of regulation directly. In our interpretations of the federal regulation of surface mining, we have drawn upon the array of state theories. This work is intended as a contribution to current debates, particularly those revolving around theses of the relative autonomy of the state and the role of the state managers. We have focused our analysis on the choices made by agency managers throughout the regulatory process and on the constraints that shape these choices.

Chapter 1 discusses the theoretical bases of the study. In the following chapter, we describe the surface mining process, its environmental consequences, and the emergence of an anti-strip mining movement. Chapter 3 examines the major controversies in the making of the federal law. In chapter 4, we analyze the formation of the regulatory agency. The process of constructing regulations is illustrated by four examples in chapter 5, and in chapters 6 and 7, we focus on the actual implementation of the regulations and on regional variations in styles of implementation. Chapter 8 explores the continuing political struggles that constrained the agency's actions. In the final chapter, we summarize our findings in light of our typological model and theories of the state. In addition, we consider several policy implications. The coda highlights some of the basic changes in regulatory policy instituted by the Reagan administration. The appendix delineates our methods of analysis.

We gratefully acknowledge the help given us by numerous people and organizations. The research was supported by a grant from the National Institute of Justice (#80–IJ–CX–0017). We also received support from the Department of Sociology and the Computer Center of the University of Tennessee. We deeply appreciate the work of our typists Betty Glenn, Carole Haimelin, Mary Jo Holden, Charlene Patrick and Teresa McMahan and of our research assistant, Stephen Groce. We are especially indebted to the scores of regulatory officials, corporate officers, and representatives of citizens' groups who generously gave of their time and knowledge in extensive interviews. Numerous people have provided us insights and corrections from their reading of various drafts of the manuscript. We benefitted from the advice given us by Bernie Auchter, Gil Geis, Ron Kramer, John Scholz, Keith Hawkins, John Thomas, Fred Block, Richard Hall, Paul Reeves, Carl Close, Norm Williams, Ed Imhoff, David Short, Bruce Boyens, Donald Crane, William Eichbaum, Carolyn Johnson, and Tom Galloway. They are not responsible, of course, for any errors that may remain or for deficiencies in interpretation.

# 1 Regulation and the State

Crime is a social construct and a legal construct. This much is commonly recognized in the popular bumper sticker, "If guns were outlawed, only outlaws would have guns." Similarly, if the production of highwalls is outlawed, only outlaws will produce highwalls. This second esoteric example is drawn from the research project described in this book. A *highwall* is a vertical surface left on a mountainside after a seam of coal has been uncovered, blasted, scooped up and hauled away. Highwalls are aesthetically unpleasing, and they contribute to dangerous mud slides and water pollution. The production of highwalls by mining firms is but one of a large number of surface mining practices outlawed by the Surface Mining Control and Reclamation Act of 1977.[1] Broadly speaking, this book is about the state's role in defining corporate crime and in regulating such illegal activities.[2] We examine the processes by which the federal government defines and regulates environmental degradation caused by the surface mining of coal.

This chapter provides a theoretical base for explaining the role of the state in defining and regulating illegal corporate behavior. In particular, we focus on a subset of such offenses—those occurring in the realm of production.

As a basis for explicating some primitive terms, let us return to our statement about highwalls: the production of highwalls was outlawed by the Surface Mining Act of 1977. We use the everyday term *outlawed* here to refer to actions that were made illegal by the passage of a law. Now law is writ, and laws are rules. They are paper threats. They represent the state's intent to regulate certain forms of behavior. But

1

laws on the books mean little in and of themselves. They are meaningful only insofar as they are backed by the mobilization of state power, law in action. The law in action entails enforcement (the mobilization of a state administrative apparatus) and sanctions (the mobilization of a state judicial apparatus). Behind these lies the state's legal (near-) monopoly of the use of force (the state's repressive apparatus).

So far we have referred only to the prohibitive or proscriptive element of law, the prohibition against leaving highwalls. But the law, of course, also prescribes, sometimes in detail. In this case, the law demands the return of mined land to "approximate original contour," and the attendant regulations (the law as administratively operationalized) specify in considerable detail the manner in which the land is to be restored.

Such prescribed detail is just one aspect of the continuous growth of the rule of law and state regulation (left-center verbiage) or state interference (right-wing version) in the economy—largely in the affairs of corporations. Corporations represent the social organization of capital, the central component of the social relations of production of modern capitalism, and the basic mechanism for the expropriation of surplus value. They are themselves creatures of the state, that is, "legal persons" designed for the protection of private property. Such "persons" are the biggest kids on the block, a fact that ought to and does make real persons a bit nervous.

## THE RISE OF REGULATION

State regulation of economic activities goes back to the origins of the state itself, if only because the social construction of "property" and "contract" as complex institutions is dependent on state power. The rise of the regulatory state, however, is concurrent with the rise of the corporation. In the United States, regulation expanded in three waves: first, around the turn of the century as a component of the Progressive Era; second, during the 1930s as part of the New Deal; and third, during the late 1960s to mid-1970s.

Current discussions of regulation make a distinction between regulation of prices and the regulation of quality (Arrow, 1981), between "old-style" economic regulation and "new-style" social regulation (Lilly and Miller, 1977), or simple between economic and social regulation (Klass and Weiss, 1978). Such distinctions are important for two reasons. First, these two types of regulatory agencies pursue different goals. Second, the two agency types vary in the authority of their legal bases, the strength of their social bases, and the orientation of their regulatory staffs. While old-style agencies focused on protection of the public interest from market imbalances,[3] the new-style agencies (such as the Office of Surface Mining) are mandated to control the social costs of production. In contrast to the earlier economic regulatory agencies, the new agencies are based on relatively stringent enabling legislation with little explicit responsibility to protect industry from economic distress.

There are now fifty-four federal regultory agencies (Chilton, 1979), and the *Code of Federal Regulations* was over 70,000 pages by 1975 (Lilly and Miller, 1977). In a purely technical sense, corporate crimes or offenses are bound to be numerous solely because of the increased volume of law. For example, the Surface Mining Act of 1977 subjected coal producers to approximately 700 regulations. In 1979 federal surface mine inspectors served over 5,000 notices of violation or cessation orders, a vast increase over the number of violations cited by the separate state agencies in previous years.

Explaining state control of the economy—how it works, for whom, by whom, why, and with what consequences—lies at the heart of our understanding of the modern world. The establishment of regulatory agencies to control the social costs of production is one of the basic forms of state intrusion into the economy. Only recently, however, have social scientists begun to provide empirical and theoretical analyses of the new regulatory agencies (e.g., Mendeloff, 1979; Wilson, 1980; Keiser, 1980; Quirk, 1980; Kelman, 1981; Menzel, 1981; Bardach and Kagan, 1982; Frank, 1983; Sabatier and Mazmonian, 1983; McCaffrey, 1982; Hawkins, 1985; Brathwaite, 1985). Since many corporate crimes are state-constructed through regulation and, at least nominally, are the objects of state control, the understanding of such offenses and their regulation hinges on larger theories of the state.

## REGULATION AND THEORIES OF THE STATE[4]

Because of their ideological centrality to our understanding of why the world is such a mess and how it ought to work, theories of the state often appear to be "essentially contested" or "incommensurable." Sharp distinctions have been drawn between pluralist versus elitist, consensus versus conflict, and mainstream liberal versus Marxist theories. Many of the disputes revolve around false polarizations.[5] We believe that the logic of a variety of neo-Marxist theories parallels the logic of some forms of non-Marxist theories. In our description of the process of regulating surface mining, we draw upon an array of theories. Our explanation of this process is synthetic. Before examining our data, we will review the major alternative arguments. We will reexamine these explanations in our final chapter.

There is one dichotomy in theories of the state and regulation that should be examined: the contrast between consensus, common good or public interest theories and special interest theories. *Public interest theories* are commonly used to describe how the state ought to function and to justify the establishment of regulatory agencies. However, such theories are rarely used to explain how the state really works (but see Sharfman, 1931). At the level of general state theory, Parsons' (1967) functional theory of the polity fits here; however, as applied to regulation, the theory has few proponents, largely because it provides no explanatory mechanisms.[6] Public interest theory tends to neglect the question of whether some strata in "the public" benefit more than others, and it downplays the importance of investigating precisely how things happen— namely, the social and political forces that produce legislative change and regulatory programs.

Nevertheless, the idea that regulation reflects the public interest is not without utility. It focuses our attention on the need for legitimation as a constraint in the production and application of regultory law and as a basis for opposition to special interests. Further, it suggests that regulatory agencies themselves, when perceived as acting in the public interest, act as legitimizers of the regulated and of the economic system as a whole. In the process, regulation is transformed into a signal that "everything is under control."

In contrast to public interest theories, alternative theories share an emphasis on special interests in shaping state policy. *Special interest theories* take three forms: weak, strong, and intermediate. The *weak* form of special interest theory is more commonly called "pluralism" (Dahl, 1967) or "countervailing power" theory (Galbraith, 1952).[7] According to the weak form of the theory, state action is determined by and for special interest groups differentially arrayed in kaleidoscopic fashion across issues and time. State policies are compromises, the results of group conflict; they reflect the weighted resources of the groups involved.[8] Many descriptions of the formation of regulatory policy fit the premises of this model (Buck, 1913; Benson, 1955; Nash, 1957; Miller, 1971 Martin, 1971).[9]

Weak form interest group theories draw our attention to forces beyond the regulatory arena that constrain the formulation and implementation of regulations. In practice, however, such approaches tend to ignore the politics of the full regulatory process. Further, the role of the state in the origin of regulations is not given sufficient attention. Finally, it is doubtful that knowledge of input (group pressure) provides a good explanation of output (the consequences of regulation).

In the *strong* form of special interest theory, the state, or some segment thereof, has been captured by a special interest group. Several varieties of special interest theory explain *capture* diversely in terms of direct control, cooptation, the development of a community of interests, or neutralization. In the "power elite" tradition, Mills (1956) and Hunter (1959) are familiar examples.[10] Among students of regulation, the thesis that agencies become the agents of the industries they were established to regulate is widely accepted by liberal theorists (McConnell, 1967; Zeigler and Peak, 1972; Salamon and Wamsley, 1976; Owen and Braeutigam, 1978).[11]

The most widely accepted strong form theories focus on incrementalism. Incremental theory holds that capture is a relatively natural consequence of the aging process (Bernstein, 1955; Downs, 1967). When the support of elected officials and broad-based public groups are lost, the agency, in quiet desperation, turns to its own clientele for support. Alternatively, once early reformers divert their attention and limited resources to other areas, the regulated industry is able to mobilize its resources more effectively to control the agency. Factors that push agencies toward capture include insufficient monetary and material resources, personnel shortages, inadequate quality of personnel, industry control of essential information and expertise, the establishment of cooperative relationships for the solution of problems, and the greater rewards for competent personnel in the regulated industry (Mitnick, 1980).

The utility of incremental capture theories is that they direct attention to change within agencies, to the constraints under which they operate, and to continuing group struggle beyond the sphere of public politics. These theories lead us to investigate the backgrounds and mobility patterns of agency personnel and to focus on changing outcomes. Deficiencies of these theories, in practice, include the lack of attention to the actual implementation of regulations and to legal-bureaucratic constraints on capture.

An *intermediate* form of special interest theory emphasizes the relative independence of politicians and/or bureaucrats in determining state policy. The roots of this perspective are found in Weber (1978) and Michels (1962): expertise, charisma of office, and control of administrative resources.[12] Most empirical studies of the regulatory process stress the importance of entrepreneurial initiatives by politicians (Landy, 1976) or bureaucrats (Weaver, 1978; Kelman, 1981; McCaffrey, 1982) in shaping policy to suit their own biases and the interests of the agency.

Radically altered in appearance by different presuppositions and vocabularies, these three forms of special interest theory appear in neo-Marxist theories of the state. In addition, Marxists have added an ultrastrong functionalist special interest theory to this array. The common component of all Marxist theories is the thesis that special interests of the capitalist class tend to predominate in state policy formulation. The theories vary in their estimates of the strength of this tendency and in their specification of the mechanisms that make it likely.

## Neo-Marxist Theories

One of the most interesting developments in recent Marxist thought has been the proliferation of theories of the state (Gold, Lo and Wright, 1975; Jessop, 1982; Carnoy, 1984). Although these theories share an emphasis on the role of the state as the "steering mechanism" for capital, they are strangely silent on the problem of state regulation of capitalist offenses. Thus, the application of neo-Marxist theories of the state to regulatory policy must be based, to some degree, on extrapolation.[13]

The source of the variety of neo-Marxist approaches is dissatisfaction with instrumentalism—the Marxist version of strong form special interest theory. *Instrumentalism,* the theory that the state is the direct instrument of the ruling class, was developed in opposition to liberal weak form theory (Domhoff, 1983; Miliband, 1969). Instrumentalism is strongly empirical in its attempt to demonstrate beyond all doubt the permanent strength of the capitalist class in the inner circle of state power. It is characterized by its specification of the explicit mechanisms, whereby the capitalist class captures the state and ensures its rule (e.g., government positions, political contributions, para-governmental policy formation organizations). Although never denying the importance of class struggle, instrumentalists tend to ignore any evidence of the effectiveness of such conflict in shaping state policy. For instrumentalists, the regulation of corporate activities is the consequence of intentional actions by "corporate liberals," enlightened capitalists from the monopoly sector who realize the need to solve crises through rationalized state intervention (Kolko, 1963, 1965; Weinstein, 1968; Domhoff, 1970, 1978).

One strength of instrumentalism is its focus on the backgrounds of agency officials and their interlinkages with capital as important influences on agency formation. Among the major complaints against instrumentalism (or direct capture theory) is its tendency to overplay the importance, and necessity, of class consciousness, direct participation, and conscious planning by elites or the capitalist class. Obversely, it underplays the significance of class struggle, of countervailing interest groups, and of the relative autonomy of the state.

It is no accident that neo-Marxist alternatives to instrumentalist theories first arose in Europe, where the paucity of capitalists in the state's inner circles and the power of state bureaucrats in determining state policy presented an anomaly that could not be ignored. The first response was a set of ultrastrong form special interest theories, reflected in the emergence of French *structuralism* (Althusser, 1970; Poulantzas, 1968, 1969) and German *state-derivationist* or *capital logic theories* (Alvater, 1977; Hirsch, 1977).[14] According to these theories, *no* intervention by capitalists is needed to ensure that the state will act to maintain the system. State policy is produced by a "relatively autonomous state" and is determined by the system, not by the capitalist class. The state's task is to resolve crises relatively independently of the conflicting demands of various fractions of capital. When the system is reproduced, the capitalist class is the special beneficiary since the system is structured for its profit.[15] These ultrastrong form theories provide functional explanations for state policy, a type of explanation that has been widely criticized for its failure to indicate any mechanisms by which the selection of functionally necessary adaptations occur (e.g., Van Parijs, 1981). Few Marxist-functionalist theories deal with the regulation of corporate activities in any detail, but they imply that any restraints imposed on particular capitalists are beneficial for capital as a whole. Such theorizing provides a general explanation for the relative independence of regulatory agencies, but often neglects the empirical question of how, specifically, the capitalist system operates through the concrete actions of state managers.

One response to the explanatory difficulties of functionalist theory has been Block's (1977, 1981) development of the *state manager theory*. In this neo-Marxist version of intermediate form special interest theory, state managers (top elected and appointed officials) are the major actors in setting state policy. Since their jobs are to steer the system, state managers will tend to be "self-interested maximizers" who establish policy beneficial to their state agency and to people like themselves. Their tendency to increase their own power at the expense of capital is constrained by states' dependence on tax revenue. State managers must attempt to set policy that is satisfying to themselves and capitalists. Policies viewed as detrimental to capital will eventually cause a "loss of business confidence" (capital strike and capital flight) and thus a loss of tax revenue. In addition, state managers must be responsive to demands of the working class (class struggle) to ensure broad support for reelection. However, since popular support is dependent on a healthy economy, state managers must maintain conditions favorable to capital accumulation.

State manager theory seems relevant for the understanding of corporate regulation since it posits state managers as being relatively autonomous from control by capitalists, except as governed by basic political-economic constraints. During periods of economic boom or crisis, managers are free to respond to class and interest group pressures in order to broaden the scope of business offenses. For example the new regulatory agencies enforce the internalization by firms of costs formerly borne externally, an impossibility under unregulated competition. Such regulation rationalizes the system by sparing "the commons" from degradation (Hardin, 1968), and it legitimates the political economy through a show of state autonomy from business.

All these previous theories tend to ignore or deny the primacy of the working class as the motor of history. Instrumentalism tends to imply the near-omnipotence of capitalists as active agents of state manipulation. Structuralist and capital logic theories place the driving forces that determine state policy beyond the power of any mere "subject." The state managerial variant does reintroduce class struggle, but only as a constraint on policy direction. Generated as an objection to these other neo-Marxist state theories, *class struggle theories* provide a more optimistic reading of the historic consequences and potential of oppositional movements (Poulantzas, 1978; Castells, 1980; Bowles and Gintis, 1982). The state is the "material condensation" of all class forces (Poulantzas, 1978:145). Because the state structure incorporates the results of previous political struggles, policy making is subject to a variety of class forces. When it is realized that contemporary notions of class struggle include the political activities of class fractions 'and even social movements having no clear economic base, it becomes clear that class struggle theories run parallel to mainstream pluralism.[16] They are the neo-Marxist version of weak form special interest theory.[17]

Despite their rising popularity, class struggle theories have rarely been applied to the analysis of state regulation. An exception is the area of occupational health and safety, where class struggle analyses have recently proliferated (Berman, 1978; Gersuny, 1981; Donnelly, 1982; Calavita, 1983).[18]

We have used components of the various theories of the state in our investigation and analysis of federal surface mining regulation. Public interest theory draws our attention to the regulatory agency's need for legitimation. Weak form interest group theory points to the role of group struggle in agency formation and operation. The strong form of the theory alerts us to factors that limit regulatory effectiveness, and the intermediate form leads us to focus on the goals, strategies, and activities of the regultory agents themselves.

## THE REGULATORY PROCESS

The regulation of surface mining, like all regulation, is the social control of activities judged detrimental to the interests of others. Regulation is an outcome of social conflict. It is the politically constructed "resolution" of social struggle. Like other forms of politics, the study of regulations involves issues of who gets what, why, when, how, and with what consequences (Lasswell, 1935; Clark, 1967). But politics is not static, nor are political disputes ever fully resolved. Regulation is a political process, not the final solution to any problem.

The answers to the question "who gets what" are deeply embedded in the answer to the question "how"—a process. Regulatory law is an attempt to formally specify constraints on how social benefits and damages will be distributed. The implementation of such law, however, subjects it to deconstruction and reconstruction at every point—the making of formal rules and less formal policy guidelines, judicial responses to litigation, the formation of an administrative structure, the establishment of enforcement procedures and implementation in the field. Previous studies of regulation have tended to focus on the question of "who gets what" by examining the content of the law itself and the consequences of regulation (beneficiaries and losers). In determining how this occurs, scholars have centered their attention on interest groups, formal bureaucratic mechanisms and high-level administrators. An emphasis on the politics of the *implementation process*—what goes on behind the administrative facade—is a notable gap in theoretical approaches to regulation.

In this study of the initial implementation of the federal surface mining law, we address the following analytical questions: (1) what are the choices available at the various points in the regulatory process, (2) what are the determinants of and limitations on such choices, and (3) what is the bearing of such choices and constraints on agency effectiveness and capture? These questions are part of the larger questions of how and why the process operates as it does.

### Choices and Constraints

Our case study of the Office of Surface Mining began with the assumption that the implementation of any regulatory program is open to a choice of options at a variety of points—that regulatory personnel enjoy considerable, but not unlimited, latitude in the construction of programs. Our task then was to discover why certain options were selected and not others. All choices have the appearance of voluntary, undetermined action, or, at least, can be viewed as largely determined by previous choices. At some level of analysis, choice must be accepted as partial explanation of action; that is, the search for determinants of choice must cease.

For the sociologist, identification of the conditions limiting choice is a useful contribution to the explanation of actions and activity patterns (e.g., agency styles). We refer to these limiting conditions as constraints. *Constraints* are social forces that channel, but do not rigidly determine, decisions and actions. Among the constraints on choice are the values and ideological biases that limit a person's willingness to "see" and "weigh" a host of alternative choices. When individuals are ensconced in a bureaucratic setting, their choices are constrained by social, economic, and political contexts and forces that narrow the consideration of options. We discuss some of these constraints later.

Our analysis of the Office of Surface Mining centers on the identification and explanation of the agency's basic style of operation. By *style* we mean the underlying pattern that is found in seemingly discrete decisions and actions and in forms of social structure. Such a style is determined by a multitude of factors. It may be established by the intent of Congress or top administrators; it may be developed through organizational drift in response to external conditions and internal dilemmas.

Since regulatory agencies are subject to contradictory pressures, it is quite possible that no clear, dominant style will emerge. When the dominant style of an agency has been established by intent, the style may be thought of as a component of a basic strategy, a fundamental plan for action. However, the dominant style could derive from a series of accidents rather than from some basic strategy. When a style is under construction and after it has been instituted, it is constantly shaped and reshaped by constraints (i.e., limiting conditions) that may reinforce, undermine, or modify it.

## STYLES OF REGULATION: A TYPOLOGICAL ANALYSIS OF THE REGULATORY PROCESS

In thinking about how a regulatory agency works, what is needed is an approach that analyzes the full regulatory process, from agenda setting to field implementation. One way to approach this task is to examine the stages of decision making and the constraints affecting such decisions, including the previous selection of options, at every stage. Our theoretical approach is typological. Each of the steps in the regulatory process entails a decision process or is the result of such a process; that is, an option taken at any point acts as a constraint on choices made at later points. For purposes of simplicity, we present polar choices at each stage of the regulatory process. Of course, such choices represent ideal types. At no point is it likely that a concrete regulatory process will fall into the most extreme category. We assume that the options selected vary across time, from law to law, from agency to agency. Further, the comparison of any concrete regulatory process with the ideal-typical model provides a starting point for the theoretical understanding of specific regulatory actions.[19]

Although numerous choices must be made at each stage of the regulatory process, many are reflections of quite distinctive yet dominant styles: enforced compliance and negotiated compliance. In its ideal-typical form, the *enforced compliance* style of regulation encompasses an overriding drive toward the rationalization of all aspects of the regulatory process. Its components include the reliance on formal, precise, and specific rules; the literal interpretation of rules; the reliance on the advice of legal technicians (attorneys); the quest for uniformity; and the distrust of and an adversarial orientation toward the regulated. The *negotiated compliance* style of regulation reflects a dominant orientation toward obtaining compliance with the spirit of the law through the use of general, flexible guidelines the discretionary interpretation of rules; bargaining between agency and regulated industry conducted by technical experts; allowance for situational factors in rule application; and an accommodative stance toward the regulated.

An advantage of this typology is that it can be tied to the fundamental question of capture versus autonomy. In general, it may be expected that selection of enforced compliance options are conducive to agency autonomy, while selection of negotiated compliance options are conducive to capture. In the enforced compliance model, the relatively autonomous legal system promotes the development of a relatively autonomous administrative apparatus for the control of the production activities of a segment of capital. Such a model fits the interests of reformers and is particularly compatible with the ideology of the new middle class, an ideology of reform through legal expertise. This model promotes the power of agency officials at the expense of specific units of capital. It is to be expected that the regulated industry generally desires a negotiated compliance approach. This approach increases the influence of the clientele in establishing the operational meaning of the law. It enhances the possibility for incremental capture of the regulatory agency.

## STAGES OF THE REGULATORY PROCESS: THE CHOICE OF OPTIONS

We focus now on selected aspects of the two polar strategies at the various stages of the regulatory process, as delineated in Table 1-1. Here and in the following sections we discuss hypothetical constraints on strategic choices.

The enabling legislation that provides the basis for any regulatory program is formulated in an arena of political conflict. When the resolution of such conflict is weighted on the side of the regulated industry, the law is likely to be vague or ambiguous concerning goals and/or appropriate means of attaining them (Bernstein, 1955); a mandate for negotiated compliance is implied, and the regulatory agency is likely to become the instrument of the "regulated." In contrast, when a political conflict is resolved in favor of an anti-industry coalition, the law is likely to be comprehensive, rigid, and precise, implying a mandate of enforced compliance (Keiser, 1980). The regulatory agency is created as an instrument of a reformist coalition, relatively autonomous from industry control. In either case, the temporary resolution of conflict in the form of law is intended as an external constraint on future agency

TABLE 1-1
**TYPOLOGY OF STYLES AND STAGES IN THE REGULATORY PROCESS**

| Stages of the Regulatory Process | Regulatory Styles | |
|---|---|---|
| | Enforced Compliance | Negotiated Compliance |
| Statute Formation | Rigid<br>Comprehensive<br>Precise | Flexible<br>Indeterminent<br>Vague |
| Bureaucratic Process | Tightly Coupled | Loosely Coupled |
| Rule Making | Adversarial<br>Formal<br>Attorney Control | Negotiational<br>Informal<br>Administrative-<br>Technical Control |
| Regulations | Legalistic<br>Detailed<br>Design Standards | Discretionary<br>Broad<br>Performance Standards |
| Rule Application | Rule-Based<br>Stringent<br>Coercive<br>Punitive | Results-Based<br>Accommodative<br>Educational<br>Conciliatory |

actions. Although it would be a mistake to assume that the regulatory process is determined solely by the structure of enabling statutes, the law may be a powerful constraint on the options selected at later stages of the regulatory process.

*Rule-making* proceedings are the initial phase in the operationalization of law. In the older economic regulatory agencies, rule making often was ad hoc, informal, and based on direct negotiation with the regulated clients. Regulatory agencies must follow a number of formal procedures in rule making, including requirements for legal justification of rules and rejected alternatives (Administrative Procedures Act) and for open public meetings (Advisory Committee Act). Under these conditions, rule making often takes on an adversarial quality, and the influence of attorneys is increased. Still, agencies are not without discretion in structuring the rule-making process. The option of selecting a relatively adversarial versus a relatively negotiational rule-making strategy remains. It is likely that selection of a more adversarial set of procedures increases the probability that the agency will establish and guard its relative autonomy.

The outcome of rule-making, regulations, is a social and political product. An agency may construct legalistic rules, precise and rigid in their demands on the regulated, or it may construct rules allowing a more discretionary approach to compliance. Legalistic rules are usually quite detailed, emphasize design standards and are intended to control industry by specifying not only *what* must be done, but exactly *how* it is to be done. Discretionary rules, by contrast, are general and stress performance standards.

Once promulgated, regulations must be implemented through a bureaucratic process—organizational structure and management style. The selection of a dominant style is not rigidly determined. Again, those who construct a regulatory bureaucracy retain a degree of latitude and discretion to structure both their internal relationships within the agency and their external relationships between more or less self-sustaining bureaucratic units.

In its relations with subunits and other agencies, we distinguish between *loosely coupled* and *tightly coupled* systems (Hagen et al., 1979). The American criminal justice system has been characterized as a weakly rationalized, loosely coupled system in which discretion is dispersed in an unsystematic manner (Hagen et al., 1979). Federal regulatory agencies may be loosely or tightly coupled with other federal agencies and with similar local agencies. The structure of a regulatory system is not wholly constrained by law, but is subject to a degree of administrative choice.

We assume that loosely coupled systems are compatible with negotiated compliance and tightly coupled systems with enforced compliance.

However constrained by the regulatory process, field agents still are faced with decisional strategies in actual rule application. A *stringent strategy* is based on criteria of uniformity, adherence to the letter of the law, and distrust of the regulated. Contrarily, *accommodative implementation practices* are based on a perceived need to take variable conditions into account and a degree of trust that the regulated will adhere to the spirit of the law. A stringent strategy is generally advanced by "tying enforcement agents to the book" (i.e., the regulations) rather than by allowing discretionary application of expertise. It seems likely that such a strategy will be associated with a coercive, rather than an educational, role model for field agents. A stringent implementation policy is intended to keep the field agents, as well as the regulated, in line.

Part of the rule application is the imposition of a scale of sanctions, which may be imposed in two ways. The punitive approach holds that violations will be limited and deterred most effectively if judgment is swift, certain, and uniform. The conciliatory approach holds that consideration of situational variables is the most effective basis for gaining compliance. The development of a rather severe set of penalties would be congruent with an ideal-typical style of enforced compliance. More symbolic kinds of punishments (or possibly, rewards) would be characteristic of a negotiated compliance style.

## CONSTRAINTS

In discussing our typology of polar options in the regulatory process, we have indicated the manner in which internal constraints (previous decisions) limit the options available at every point. Real choice is limited further by an array of external constraints, particularly: the state of the economy, political forces, and available resources.

Regulatory agencies are constrained by the state of the economy. In general, economic regulation seems to be the result of class conflict in "hard times." Such regulation reformulates and legitimates the economic system; in addition, it legitimates the role of the state as the protector of the public interest. Support for economic regulatory agencies apparently is subject to gradual erosion (delegitimation) in periods of prosperity and, thus, to demands for deregulation in succeeding periods of stagnation or decline. The regulation of products and the production process seems to be a result of the class politics of relatively prosperous times. Initially such regulation also legitimates a reformed economic system and the role of the state. As social regulation contributes to the fiscal crisis of the state, it may lose its legitimating function. Since this new regulation appears to limit economic growth, economic stagnation pushes social regulators toward policies of increased negotiated compliance.

If politics is defined in its broadest sense as all attempts to influence or control state policy, then political forces act as external constraints on state agencies at every step of the regulatory process. In the case of the old economic regulatory agencies, oppositional groups tended to withdraw to the sidelines after the passage of an already weak act. In the case of the new social regulatory agencies, this withdrawal has not yet occurred (Sabatier, 1975). The shaping of the regulatory process within these new agencies is subject to the external constraint of continuing political pressures. These political forces include reformist organizations, the regulated industries (usually somewhat divided along monopoly capital and competitive capital lines), the states, Congress, and the courts. Reformists usually press for enforced compliance policies, while states and industries usually press for negotiated compliance strategies—competitive capital more so than monopoly capital. Although the courts typically support any agency action that follows legal procedures, they and Congress may swing either way.

Finally, the availability of resources is a determinant of agency policies. Insufficient budgets, inadequate personnel (in terms of either quantity or quality), and lack of adequate information tend to push agencies toward adopting negotiated compliance strategies.

In the following chapters, we employ our interpretive typological schema to describe and analyze the creation, implementation, and impact of the federal government's attempt to regulate the surface coal mining industry. In a concluding chapter, we return to our theoretical typology in a more explicit manner and discuss policy implications in light of this approach.

# 2  Surface Mining and the Environment

Nearly 25 percent of the world's recoverable coal deposits are found in the United States. Given the present economics and technology of mining, about one-half of america's 474.6 billion tons of coal reserves is recoverable (U.S. Department of Energy, 1982:137). Little wonder that since the oil embargo of the early 1970s, many politicians and coal industry spokesmen have referred to the United States as the "Saudi Arabia of coal" and have called for greater reliance on coal as an energy source.

## TRENDS IN AMERICAN COAL PRODUCTION

For 200 years, coal was mined almost exclusively by underground or *deep mining* methods. From combinations of shafts and tunnels, miners blasted and gouged the coal from its natural strata or *seams*. After loading onto conveyances of various kinds, the coal was hauled to the surface for processing and shipping. In 1920 approximately 98 percent of the coal produced in America came from deep mines. In 1950 deep mining still accounted for 76 percent of American production (President's Commission on Coal, 1980). Nearly all of this coal was extracted from Appalachia.

Two recent developments have altered drastically the traditional patterns of American coal mining: the expansion of surface mining and the increasing importance of western coal production. In the late 1950s and early 1960s, surface coal production rapidly began claiming a larger share of U.S. coal production. As a result, by 1970 surface mining methods accounted for 45 percent of U.S. coal production; by 1980 this had risen to 59 percent (U.S. Department of Energy, 1982:125).

The major reasons for the expansion of surface mining are economic. Net production costs for surface-mined coal are lower than for deep-mined coal, and the average surface miner produces approximately three times more coal per day than the average deep miner. Surface mining can recover up to 90 percent of the coal in a seam, while deep mining recovers less than 60 percent (U.S. Department of Energy, 1980:7). Also, the development of surface mining has been spurred by dramatic increases in the size and handling capacity of heavy equipment.

Although coal is found beneath thirty-one states, coal deposits cluster in three regions of the United States: Appalachia, the Midwest, and the West. The geographical distribution of American coal is depicted graphically in Figure 2–1.

Historically, the lion's share of coal production occurred east of the Mississippi River. In 1970, 92 percent of the coal produced came from mines located in the East, largely from Appalachia. However, by 1980 only 62 percent of American coal production came from eastern mines (U.S. Department of Energy, 1983:125). In Appalachia thousands of firms, many of them quite small, engage in surface mining. On steep mountain slopes and in narrow valleys, they mine relatively thin seams of high energy, high sulfur coal.

The midwestern region is more hospitable to coal operators because of its gently rolling farmlands, its moderate rainfall, its thicker coal seams, and its lower overburden ratio. These advantages permit the use of much larger machinery than is possible in most of Appalachia. Midwestern and Appalachian coal is primarily bituminous.

Thicker seams and thinner overburden combine to make western mining highly profitable. Western coal has a low sulfur content, which accounts for much of the increased western production since passage of the 1970 Clean Air Act. Western surface mines tend to be extremely large. In marked contrast with Appalachia, there are only a few hundred mines west of the Mississippi River. In 1979, 43 percent of total Appalachian coal production was mined by surface methods, while the comparable percentage for western production was 89 percent (U.S. Department of Energy, 1981:7).

## THE SURFACE COAL MINING PROCESS

The technical process of surface coal mining can be comprehended easily. A somewhat idyllic description is provided by the National Coal Association:

Figure 2-1
Geographical Distribution of Coal in the United States

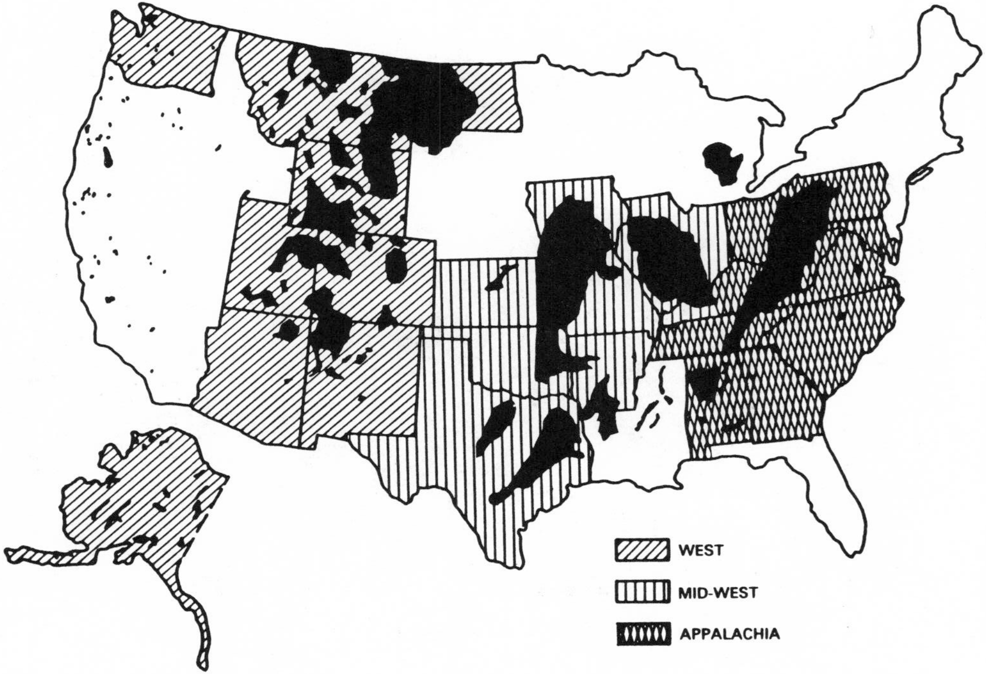

WEST
MID-WEST
APPALACHIA

> [T]he coal is produced . . . from seams lying fairly close to the earth's surface. The earth and rock above the coal seam—the overburden—are removed and placed to one side; the exposed coal is broken up, loaded into trucks and hauled away. Bulldozers then grade the overburden to the desired shape, the surface is replanted with seeds or your trees, and the land is restored to productive use. [*Coal Facts,* 1976:11]

There are two principal methods employed in surface coal mining: contour mining and area mining. *Contour mining* is the most common method of surface mining in the mountainous regions of Appalachia. In this process, bulldozers cut a shelf, or *bench,* into the side of the mountain. The vertical wall created by the bench cut is referred to as the highwall; the undisturbed portion of the mountain below the bench is the *downslope.* Explosives, placed in the highwall, are used to loosen the overburden. After the loosened overburden, or *spoil,* is removed, the coal is loaded onto trucks and hauled away for processing. The mining proces continues by extending the bench cut along the contour of the mountain. Figure 2-2 illustrates the removal of coal using contour mining techniques.

Because of the relatively flat terrain, surface mining in midwestern and western coal regions employs *area mining* techniques (see Figure 2-3). In this process, the overburden is removed with very large shovels suspended from booms. An initial trench is dug to reach the coal seam, and the spoil is placed beside the trench. As subsequent, parallel trenches are dug, the spoil materials are placed into the adjacent, previously mined trench. Successive trenches are made until the entire coal seam is excavated.

## THE DESTRUCTIVE EFFECTS OF EARLY SURFACE COAL MINING

Until passage of the Surface Mining Control and Reclamation Act of 1977, regulation of surface coal mining was left to the states. Though the earliest law (West Virginia) was enacted in the late 1930s, state laws, regulations, and regulatory agencies were woefully inadequate. Statutes and regulations were weak, enforcement was lax and, in some states, corrupt. Partly in response to the threat of federal intervention, most states began to strengthen their regulatory laws by the early 1970s (Imhoff, Friz and LaFevers, 1976). In most states, particularly in Appalachia, these laws were not enforced vigorously (Save Our Cumberland Mountains, 1978).

Figure 2-2
Surface Mining—Contour Method

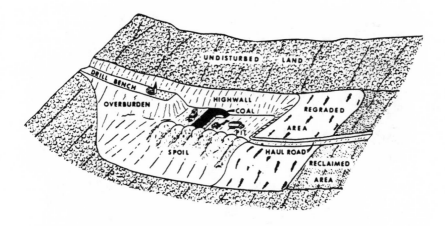

1. Topsoil is removed and stockpiled for later reclamation purposes.
2. A bench is dozed into the side of the slope.
3. Blasting cracks the dense overburden.
4. Overburden is hauled by scrapers or trucks and is backfilled continuously.
5. Coal is removed by loaders and/or shovels and carried out of the mining area along the haul road (which has been cut into the slope).
6. While blasting for the next stage of overburden removal, reclamation of the first cut is beginning: the pit is filled with overburden, regraded, layered with topsoil, then seeded.

SOURCE: The President's Commission on Coal 1980:159

In Appalachia, the years before the late 1970s are often referred to as the era of "shoot 'n' shove" mining. This richly evocative label calls attention to the routine, but socially and environmentally harmful, mining practices of those times. The easiest and cheapest mining methods were used, with little regard to the social and environmental impacts; for example, explosives often were used recklessly and, in the process, nearby residents and their dwellings were subjected to rock and other debris (flyrock) hurled from the explosions. In Appalachia spoil materials usually were shoved over the side of the mountain—a practice known as "pushing spoil over the downslope."

The absence of effective state regulation not only permitted harmful mining practices, but also enabled many operators to abandon depleted or unprofitable mine sites without any reclamation. By the mid-1960s, nearly one million acres had been left in this unreclaimed condition (U.S. Department of the Interior, 1967). Consequently, the highly unstable and acidic spoil materials were left to erode under the onslaught of

Figure 2-3
Surface Mining—Area Method

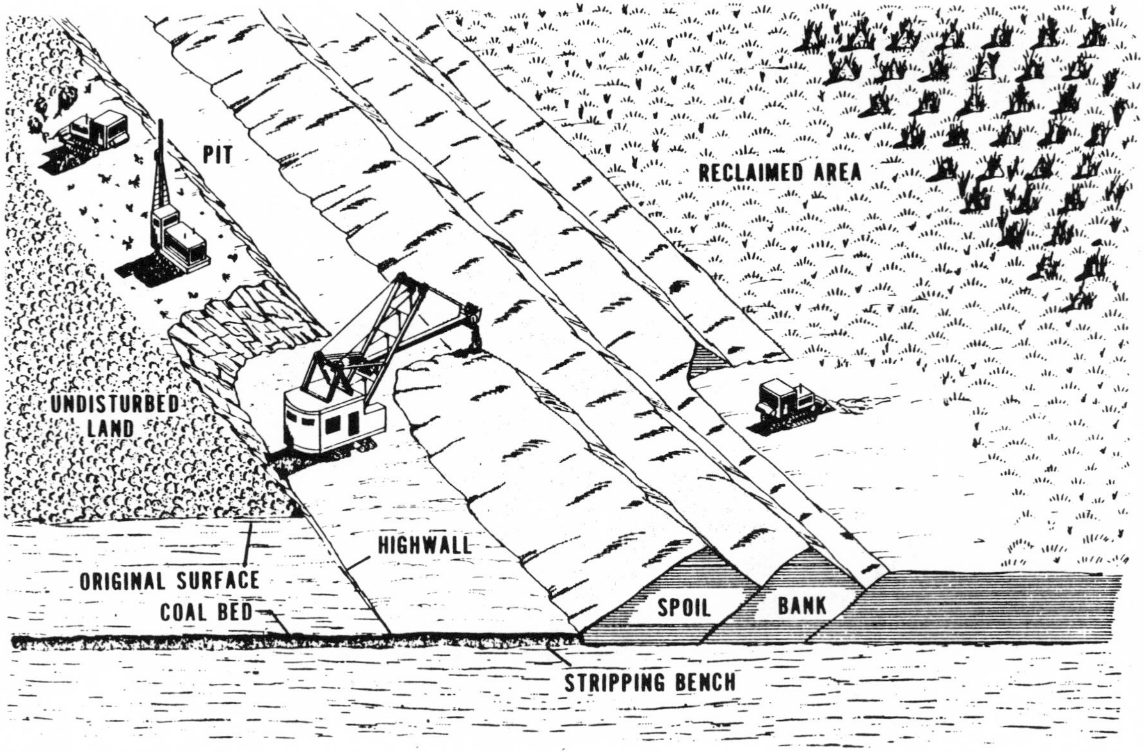

SOURCE: Grim and Hill 1974:30

rains. The resulting sedimentation and acidic runoff choked streams, caused floods and mudslides, killed aquatic life, and ruined wells and other water supplies, especially in Appalachia. After the passage of several years, many spoil banks achieved a degree of stability, but they often would not support vegetation.

By the 1960s, a surge of published work by popular writers (e.g., Caudill, 1962) and by government agencies (e.g., U.S. Department of the Interior, 1967) called attention to the environmental destruction caused by such mining practices. Rendered useless because of inadequate reclamation or abandonment, portions of the American landscape resembled the surface of the moon. In the Midwest and in Appalachia, indigenous citizens' groups and landowners were becoming more vocal in their call for tough regulation of the surface mining industry. The marriage of these indigenous protest groups with the environmentalist movement gave new impetus to the demand for effective regulatory legislation.

## THE ANTI-STRIP MINING MOVEMENT

Vigorous opposition to strip mining arose in the latter half of the 1960s in Appalachia (Fisher and Foster, 1979) and in the early 1970s in the West. Discouraged by the ineffectiveness of state laws (Schneider, 1971; Munn, 1975) and the difficulty of mountain reclamation, Appalachian citizens' groups overwhelmingly favored the abolition of strip mining. The grass roots anti-stripping movement engaged in sit-ins on strip mine sites, occasionally sabotaged mining equipment, took its case to the courts, and tried to change state laws. However, its resources were few, its membership base was thin, and budgets slim. Its local constituent groups were only loosely coordinated, and political, legal, and technical expertise was limited.

Constraints on the success of the movement were great. Most Appalachian coal is in the hands of absentee owners (Appalachian Land Ownership Task Force, 1983). However, most of the coal is mined by local operators, who are protected by local politicians with mining interests. Even *wildcatting* (mining without a permit) was virtually impossible to prosecute successfully because of the collusion of mine operators and the "courthouse crowd." Additionally, in most of the Appalachian states, the worst abuses of surface mining were carried out in remote areas, whose residents had little political clout in the state legislatures. Faced with these difficulties, the movement quickly sought federal relief.

In the West, massive surface mining arose very rapidly in the 1970s. Most of the mining was done by the largest coal companies on land leased from the federal government. State governments moved quickly to regulate mining and to get their share of the new wealth. Western state regulations were strict in comparison to those in the East. Still, opposition groups soon emerged around the issues of property rights, the loss of agricultural and grazing lands, and the very possibility of reclamation in arid regions. In both the Midwest and Far West, local rights groups and farmers provided strong support for a federal surface mining law.

The major success of the grass roots organizations was in publicizing the nature and extent of surface mining as an environmental issue. The issue appealed to the media, already attuned to environmental problems. Thus, strip mining, a spectacular example of ecological abuse, became a national issue in the hands of the larger environmental movement.

What was the nature of this movement? Who were these environmentalists? What resources did they bring to the battle? Historically, environmentalism in the United States has its roots in the conservationist movement of the late nineteenth century. When the environmental movement emerged as a political force in the late 1960s, its organizational base included the older conservationist groups (e.g., National Audubon Society and the Sierra Club) and some newer, more activist associations (e.g., Friends of the Earth and the National Resources Defense Council). By the mid-1970s, environmentalist organizations had a combined membership of between four and five million (Mitchell, 1979; Humphrey and Buttel, 1982). As in the case of the early movement (Reiger, 1975), research indicates that the membership base of these organizations was solidly upper-middle class (Harry et al., 1969; Devell, 1970; Faich and Gale, 1971; Harry, 1974).[1] This social base provided the environmentalist movement with a wide array of resources: legal and technical knowledge, communication and organizational skills, personnel ties to politicians and state managers, and money.

The national environmentalist organizations—there also are thousands of smaller local groups—are "funded social movement organizations" (McCarthy and Zald, 1973). Their policies are constructed and carried out by a small band of professional leaders supported by a "dues constituency." The latter also may be thought of as a "conscience constituency," in the sense that the payoff for contributions is indirect. The passage of numerous environmental laws—the National Environmental Policy Act, the Clean Air Act, the Federal Water Pollution Act, and the Coastal Zone Management Act—testifies to the effectiveness of lobbying by funded social movement organizations. Environmental organizations also bear the brunt of sponsoring litigation meant to insure that laws will be enforced in the public interest (Handler, 1978). It is with some justification that environmentalist groups claim to stand for the public interest. During the late 1960s, concern for environmental quality rose from nowhere to second place among public issues (Erskine, 1972).[2]

When the national environmental organizations joined the fray for surface mining reform, they possessed many resources needed for a long battle. They brought a record of legislative and lobbying success, a moderate financial base, a public mobilized for further reform action, and considerable legal and technical skill. The nine national environmental organizations that testified in the 1971–1972 congressional hearings on surface mining legislation represented approximately one-half million people. By 1973–1974 their activities were coordinated with those of a number of local groups in a Coalition Against Strip Mining— twenty-six organizations overall, representing ranchers, farmers, Native Americans, sportspersons, churches, and environmentalists. As the activities and goals of these organizations coalesced, the Environmental Policy Center was founded in Washington, D.C., and became the major lobbying organization for congressional action.

The struggle for reform was led by a handful of young coordinators and lobbyists. They were backed by an array of citizens' groups and funded by environmentalist organizations and foundation. The desire of the grass roots groups for the abolition of surface mining was compromised almost from the beginning of the battle, a strategic choice that led to a certain amount of internal conflict. During the long march toward federal regulation, the leaders honed their political, legal, and technical skills. Later, these skills enabled them to help shape a tightly-drawn law that could be used to limit the discretionary power of the proposed federal regulatory agency.

# 3   The Battle to Enact Legislation

Federal surface mining legislation was supported by environmentalists, conservationists, and grass roots groups. Legislative proposals ranged from total prohibition of strip mining to severe restrictions on the places where, and the conditions under which, it could be conducted. Arrayed against this coalition were the coal industry, manufacturers of heavy equipment, and the electric utilities. In their nine-year effort to block federal legislation, the industry consistently put forth the same set of objections.

## NINETIETH CONGRESS (1968): HEARINGS

In 1968 congressional testimony, coal industry representatives opposed any federal effort to regulate surface coal mining. Industry representatives admitted that strip mining had produced environmental and property damage; however, past damages were portrayed as the negligent practices of a few irresponsible operators who, for the most part, were no longer mining coal. The American Mining Congress (AMC) testified that the problems "have been recognized and are being dealt with by the States in which they exist; there is no indication that additional controls are needed' (U.S. Congress, Senate, 1968:99). In addition, it argued that

> establishment of [federal] guidelines or standards is especially difficult because every mining operation is to some extent unique, and what would be inconsistent with good mining practices in the desert

country of the sparsely settled areas of the West might be unacceptable in the East where rainfall and the nature of alternative land uses create far different conditions. [U.S. Congress, Senate, 1968:104]

The AMC representative assured the senators that the mining industry had been "actively engaged for years . . . to minimize side effects of mining operations" (U.S. Congress, Senate, 1968:97). Similarly, one of the nation's largest coal companies assured the congressional committee that

the industry today has the technical and engineering staffs to reclaim strip mined land—and they are doing the job—emphatically so! Remarkable progress has been made in the art of land reclamation in the last few years. This progress has been made under local and state supervision, and it is now in good hands. [U.S. Congress, Senate, 1968:135]

Those who testified in favor of some type of federal surface mining statute were divided, especially on the question of the adequacy of state reclamation laws. Harry Caudill, a former Kentucky legislator and the author of *Night Comes To The Cumberlands* (1963) and *My Land Is Dying* (1971), urged the senators to "view with caution and skepticism industry claims that present State laws are working well and that voluntary efforts are handling the problems satisfactorily (U.S. Congress, Senate, 1968:92). Others were less critical of state efforts. One witness, for example, told the committee that "new and strong state laws are all fairly recent, and the time to see whether they are going to be sufficient without further public action has not yet passed" (U.S. Congress, Senate, 1968:338).

This tendency to defer to state regulation was supported by the states themselves. Oklahoma's governor informed the committee by letter that "all segments of the mining industry in Oklahoma have shown their willingness to cooperate in implementation of our reclamation law. I see no reason to add additional burdens to the State by passing Federal reclamation legislation" (U.S. Congress, Senate, 1968:287). Georgia's chief geologist assured the senators that "in the light of the legislation to control surface mining passed by the 1968 session of the Georgia General Assembly, we see no need or justification for [federal legislation]" (U.S. Congress, Senate, 1968:326).

Two points assumed importance later. First, a number of senators and witnesses suggested that the states were reluctant to develop strong regulatory programs for fear of harming local mining interests. It was argued that a federal law, by equalizing the regulatory costs, would eliminate any competitive advantage for a state with weak laws. Nonetheless, Wyoming's governor told the committee: "Surface mining regulation should not be used to equalize competitive situations. It should be limited to its stated purpose—to conserve natural resources" (U.S. Congress, Senate, 1968:351). The western governors recognized, in the words of Montana's Tim Babcock, that they were standing "on the threshold of development of great coal deposits" (U.S. Congress, Senate, 1968:346). Wyoming's Stanley Hathaway told the committee that states with comparable surface mining problems should be "allowed the opportunity to cooperate regionally in solving their problems" (U.S. Congress, Senate, 1968:352).

The second issue was raised briefly during the 1968 hearings by the National Association of Manufacturers (NAM): "A perpetual, overhanging possibility of federal intervention [was that it] . . . would make realistic planning—from both the operational and economic standpoints—practically impossible" (U.S. Congress, Senate, 1968:307). The NAM was suggesting that the uncertainty about federal regulatory legislation could prove damaging to the mining industry, quite apart from the substance of regulations themselves.

## INTERIM EVENTS

The Senate Interior Committee did not report a bill in the Ninetieth Congress, and further hearings were not held until 1971. In the interim, there was a dramatic increase in the pace and volume of state regulatory legislation. Between 1965 and 1977, thirty-eight states either enacted or amended their strip mining laws.

The states also made a limited cooperative effort to cope with strip mining problems by establishing the Interstate Mining Compact Commission (IMCC). Conceived in 1964 at the Southern Governors' Conference, the IMCC was organized to prod the mining industry "to utilize techniques designed to minimize waste of our natural resources" and to take action "to assure adherence to sound standards and procedures by the mining industry" (*IMCC, Annual Report,* 1978, 1979:6). Currently there are seventeen member states and all but three (Texas, Oklahoma, and New Mexico) are located in either the midwestern or Appalachian regions (IMCC, 1981). During the Commission's organizational period, it noted:

> Many states have failed to pass adequate legislation for the protection of their lands and water and because of this the federal government has now undertaken the task of writing a law that will apply nationwide. Had the Compact become active a few years earlier, there would be no need for federal legislation in this field for it is required that each state pass adequate surface mining legislation in order to become a member of the Compact. [IMCC, n.d.: 3-4]

The IMCC movement was "too little, too late" and may have foundered because of regional competition for coal markets. Some states apparently felt they had little to gain through tough regulations since their reclamation and existing environmental problems were not as severe as those in other regions, chiefly Appalachia. In any case, none of the western states with large mining reserves has elected to join the IMCC.

Certainly, midwestern and eastern coal operators fear western competition. A 1974 study notes: "Midwestern coal markets have declined in recent years. . . . A part of the regional demand for Midwestern coal has been transferred to the Northern Great Plains where extensive low-sulfur coal reserves are currently being developed" (Carter et al., 1974:5). The president of the Harlan County (Kentucky) and National Independent Coal Operators' Association expressed concern about western coal invading traditional markets for eastern coal. He suggested forming an "operators' league to promote the use of Appalachian coal," saying that "if we don't unite our efforts together [sic] and offset some of the Western strippers," the eastern coal industry may be severely damaged (National Independent Coal Leader, April 1977:21).

## NINETY-SECOND AND NINETY-THIRD CONGRESSES: HEARINGS AND LEGISLATION

By 1971 hope that the states could and would regulate surface mining had all but disappeared. In the Ninety-second and Ninety-third Congresses, approximately twenty bills to regulate strip mining were introduced and committee hearings were held. A witness for Save Our Kentucky, a citizens' group opposing strip mining, told the House committee that

> Kentucky's reclamation attempts have been a whole-sale failure. Reclamation is a fiction. It is the grandest lie perpetuated upon the American public. The so-called reclamation which the strippers practice does not even merit the description of repair work. [U.S. Congress, House, 1972:541]

Replacing 1968's cautiously optimistic view was the firm conviction by legislation supporters that strip mining would have to be banned entirely or, failing that, the job of regulating it turned over to the federal government. The former deputy director of West Virginia's Department of Natural Resources told the Senate Committee:

> [T]he surface mining industry in Appalachia is not amenable to social control. . . . In a word, State regulation is no match for the surface mine industry, at least in West Virginia. [U.S. Congress, Senate, 1972: 285,287]

The witness doubted that a federal law would make any appreciable difference, but he noted such a law would have some advantages.

> [A]t least it offers escape from the depressing game of economic blackmail which has so frequently reduced State legislatures and State regulatory bodies to virtual impotence. [U.S. Congress, Senate, 1972:287]

Environmental, conservationist, and landowner groups were not completely united during the 1971–1973 hearings; their proposals took both "hard" and "soft" positions. The hard position called for an end to all strip mining, commencing from six to eighteen months after enactment of legislation. The soft position advocated a ban on strip mining only in areas or locations where adequate reclamation was not possible. A variation of the soft position called for the abolition of certain types of strip mining, primarily contour stripping in mountainous regions. Supporters of both hard and soft positions maintained that deep mining could be stimulated sufficiently to minimize any temporary decrease in coal production.

In a reversal of its 1968 position opposing all federal legislation, the coal industry now supported minimum federal guidelines for regulating surface mining. Coal representatives advocated that the states be given the opportunity to develop regulations consistent with national guidelines and that the federal government enforce federal regulations only in states that failed to develop an acceptable regulatory program. The president of the National Coal Association told the Senate committee that

> [t]he *responsible companies* of the coal industry now support reasonable Federal legislation which will enable the States to do a more effective job of regulating surface mining and reclamation. We

believe fair and reasonable regulation, uniformly enforced, can and will allow the continued production of coal for the national interest and will assure that all operators—*including some who might otherwise shirk their duty, to the detriment of the whole industry and the Nation*—follow good reclamation practice. [U.S. Congress, Senate, 1972:315; emphasis added]

Although less enthusiastic, the National Independent Coal Operators' Association supported the NCA's position (U.S. Congress, Senate, 1972:775–77). On the other hand, the Tri-County Independent Coal Operators—which represented smaller Virginia operators—continued to oppose federal legislation, generally making the argument that the states were adequate to the task (U.S. Congress, Senate, 1972:619–23).

The industry's "support" of federal legislation hardly could be called enthusiastic. To a large extent, it publicly endorsed the concept of federal controls as a means to offset the extreme measures strip mining opponents demanded. Moreover, the industry asserted that it would support only "workable, reasonable, and realistic" legislation. Over the next six years, the industry offered nominal support for federal legislation, but stressed the need for flexible guidelines.

The record suggests that the largest coal producers were concerned primarily with protecting, if not enhancing, the value of their western coal leases. As such, they sought to allay the concerns of western lawmakers who did not want their states to become another Appalachia. The basic goal of large coal in nominally supporting federal legislation was to ensure that the law would be sufficiently flexible to accommodate site-specific mining variations. In addition, such support was a mechanism for pressuring "irresponsible" elements in the industry to put more effort into reclamation.

The 1971–1973 congressional hearings were critical for the coal industry. In emphasizing its support for "fair, realistic, and reasonable" federal legislation, the coal industry advanced eight key points:

(1) Because of the immense diversity in mining conditions and problems in the fifty states, federal regulations would have to be broad and flexible, rather than specific and rigid.

(2) The environmental abuses of strip mining were a product of the past and were produced by a small percentage of operators, those on the fringe of the industry. Comparable abuses could not and would not occur again.

(3) Environmental abuses would not continue because the "science" of reclamation was so much more developed than in earlier times. In

fact developments in reclamation technology were taking place at such a fast pace that virtually all land would be reclaimable in the future.

(4) A total ban on strip mining would reduce coal production, make the United States more dependent on foreign fuels, and lead to electric power shortages.

(5) A total ban on strip mining would produce rising unemployment and have a severe economic effect in areas dependent on coal mining.

(6) A rapid or substantial conversion to underground mining could not prevent these consequences because the lead time required to open deep mines was too long.

(7) A return to deep mining would consign increasing numbers of miners to death or injury.

(8) The federal government should play a larger part in supporting and conducting coal-related research.

The industry generally avoided taking a rigid stance on any single aspect of the debated bills. It called for flexibility only in those areas where it would increase its options in planning and conducting mining activities. It opposed flexibility in legislative provisions that would decrease its own operating options or increase unpredictability. The industry, for example, urged narrow, inflexible provisions for public comment on mining permit applications and for citizen suits against coal operators. Similarly, industry representatives generally opposed the inclusion of criminal sanctions in federal legislation.

> [I]n matters affecting mined land where every operation is necessarily unique, it is most unfair to suggest that operators should be subject to criminal sanctions when the regulations issued pursuant to the act will be couched in generalized language. The proper enforcement mechanism in such situations is by way of injunction, the terms of which will explicitly define the impact of the regulation in a specific mining operation. [U.S. Congress, Senate, 1972:283]

The importance of allaying western lawmakers' anxieties cannot be overestimated. In 1972, 77 percent of the House committee members and all of the Senate committee members were from the West. Arizona's Senator Paul Fannin told Tennessee's Senator Howard Baker that he had seen the damage done by stripping in Appalachia and stated, "I don't want that to happen to my State" (U.S. Congress, Senate, 1972:586).

Also, the constituents of some western lawmakers resisted the encroachment of surface coal mining. A Montana witness told the Senate Committee:

> We do not want our beautiful State of Montana ruined, nor other Western States, in order to decrease the air pollution in the East when the true motive behind strip mining is a higher margin of profit for the coal companies. This greed and irresponsibility of the coal companies will lead to the destruction of our area and others like it. [U.S. Congress, Senate, 1972:646]

The coal industry was successful in the 1971–1973 session in defeating the call for a ban on strip mining. In general, the industry appeared to convince western lawmakers that their region was sufficiently different from Appalachia that they need not worry. Moreover, the industry was successful in its efforts to persuade the congressional committees that abolition of strip mining would be catastrophic, as the final committee report demonstrates:

> The Committee is aware of the critical energy situation facing the nation and the very significant role that coal plays in the energy supply picture. This was a significant factor in directing the Committee's attention to means for regulation and control of coal mining surface activities rather than outright prohibition. The latter would create an intolerable situation in the presently overstrained energy supply picture. [U.S. Congress, Senate, 1972:19]

The committee further expressed its concern about the economic and employment problems that would result from a ban on strip mining and declared its belief that reclamation not only was possible, but that first-rate reclamation work was being conducted. Although the House did pass a bill (H.R. 6482), the Ninety-second Congress did not enact surface coal mining legislation.

## NINETY-THIRD AND NINETY-FOURTH CONGRESSES: LEGISLATION AND VETOES

Gerald Ford's opposition to strip mining legislation was well known; consequently, the coal industry could stall as long as Ford occupied the White House. From 1971 to the passage of the Surface Mining Act in 1977, the industry supported the concept of federal controls, but worked to defeat any specific bill. Its 1971–1973 testimony and the oil embargo of 1973 served to put advocates of strong strip mining controls in a defensive position. In 1974 the bill that passed the Ninety-third Congress (S. 425) was modified to deal with the industry's contentions that regulation led to increased unemployment. S. 425 contained sections providing extra unemployment benefits for anyone put out of work by surface mine shutdowns resulting from federal controls and giving preference in reclamation contracts to former mine operators or employees who possessed the requisite heavy equipment (U.S. Congress, Senate, 1974). Still, the industry was not entirely happy. For one thing, the bill contained provisions permitting the secretary of interior to designate lands unsuitable for mining, and the industry opposed such flat prohibitions.

President Ford vetoed S. 425 in late 1974, and Congress responded by passing a similar 1975 bill (H.R. 25), which Ford also vetoed. Ford's opposition to the two surface mining bills hinged on (1) the unemployment the bills would cause, (2) higher electricity costs for consumers, (3) an increasing American dependence on foreign oil, and (4) the resulting decrease in coal production (U.S. Congress, House, 1975).

## NINETY-FIFTH CONGRESS: THE SURFACE MINING CONTROL AND RECLAMATION ACT OF 1977

Angered by Ford's rationales for vetoing the 1975 bill, congressional committees introduced the Surface Mining Control and Reclamation Act of 1977 as the second bill in the House and the seventh bill in the Senate. The nation's continuing energy problems strengthened the industry's position that nothing should be done to handicap surface mining. Economic developments, however, made the industry more willing to accept federal controls. Uncertainty about federal coal mining regulations was making it difficult for the industry to attract external capital and, thus, to plan mining ventures. Colorado's Governor Richard Lamm indicated that in the West

> one of the problems we have . . . is the whole question of predictability . . . and what we would like [is] some overall idea about where the impact is going to take place so that we can react to it and anticipate. [U.S. Congress, Senate, 1972:101–2]

The industry realized it could no longer count on a sympathetic presidential veto when candidate Jimmy Carter stated his support for surface mining regulation. According to *Coal Age* (December 1976:21), Carter was convinced that "substantial increases in coal production and utilization will only come with a stable regulatory climate. The veto of the strip mining bill merely prolonged the climate of uncertainty."

Although by 1977 passage of legislation was a foregone conclusion, there remained groups and individuals who wanted to contest issues that were then moot. They had not heard the message that Congress no longer was considering a total ban on strip mining. The president of Save Our Cumberland Mountains told the House subcommittee, "We feel that the only sensible thing is to start a regulated phase out of strip mining" (U.S. Congress, House, 1977:29). Others wanted to contest the issue of whether mined land could be reclaimed, apparently not realizing that Congress already had accepted the industry's assurances that the "science of reclamation" was progressing daily. A Montana cattle rancher called this a "dangerous premise," arguing that

> reclamation research is a new form of alchemy. Although old-time alchemists abandoned the idea of turning base metals into gold, the present-day reclamation alchemists are now faced with transforming money and spoil material into diverse vegetative forage.
> The saddest aspect . . . is that the reclaimers and researchers and the general public desperately want to believe the new alchemic theory, because it rationalizes the advisability of strip mining. [U.S. Congress, Senate, 1972:51]

Members of the House and Senate subcommittee assured industry representatives that they wanted to write a bill that would increase U.S. coal production. Arizona's Representative Morris Udall told a utility company representative:

> I want to assure you that I believe the Nation has got to increase the production of coal over the next decade. It is our insurance policy against the Arabs. . . . I want to write [a bill] that lets more coal be mined and lets it be mined at a reasonable cost . . . but this uncertainty is paralyzing the country. [U.S. Congress, Senate, 1972:49]

Although the entire coal industry opposed the 1977 bill (H.R. 2), a division of interest emerged between eastern and western coal producers. These two segments of the industry differed in the adamance and extent of their opposition to the bill. Western witnesses made statements of opposition in an obligatory fashion, but then went on to offer detailed amendments. Western operators were concerned about prohibitions on mining on alluvial valley floors, provisions for acquiring surface owner consent to mine, and restrictions on the length of mining permits and the permit renewal process. These issues did not concern eastern operators who were more vociferous—even defiant—in their statements of opposition. Generally eastern operators were fearful that the bills' provisions for returning mined land to its approximate original contour would make it (1) effectively impossible to mine much eastern coal and (2) too costly for small operators to comply. However, both industry segments were united in their call for amendments to provisions governing citizen suits, public hearings, and requirements for determining the hydrological consequences of surface mining.

In their testimony, the coal industry consistently sought to increase their options under the forthcoming bill, while limiting any opposition. Industry saw citizen suits and public hearings on applications for mining permits as potential sources of harassment and, therefore, delay and unpredictability. With respect to citizen suits, Congressman Udall reassured a witness:

> One of the most utter frustrations of people who fear coal mining in Appalachia is that there is no one to talk to. The legislature has been bought off, in their view, and at the county courthouse the judge and all the lawyers are on the side of the coal companies. If they had some place to be heard and take out their frustrations, a lot of times that helps. You give your wife the right to complain and sometimes she won't complain. They don't have a forum to be heard, and that is the philosophy behind the citizen suit provisions, to legitimize and standardize some kind of forum through which people who haven't been heard on the strip mining provision could be heard. [U.S. Congress, Senate, 1972:50]

Despite industry opposition, the Surface Mining Control and Reclamation Act passed both Houses of Congress and was signed by President Carter in August, 1977.

## OVERVIEW OF THE ACT

The Surface Mining Control and Reclamation Act of 1977 (SMCRA) has been reviewed and discussed elsewhere (e.g., Eichbaum and Babcock, 1982; Dale, 1978; Harvey, 1978). The eighty-eight-page act provides for a national regulatory program "to prevent or mitigate adverse environmental effects of present and future coal mining operations." Here we present an overview of the act to make readers familiar with its more important provisions. In subsequent chapters, we examine these provisions in more detail.

In stating the act's rationale, Congress asserted its belief that (1) technology is available to reclaim the economic and environmental impacts of surface coal mining, and (2) regulatory efforts should be focused at the state level. Toward that end, the Office of Surface Mining Reclamation and Enforcement (OSM) was established in the Department of Interior and empowered to promulgate and enforce surface coal mining regulations in conjunction with existing state programs. Eventually the states, by incorporating the standards mandated in the act and specified in the regulations, would assume primary regulatory responsibility, with the OSM functioning in an oversight capacity.

The new agency was required to publish a final set of interim regulations by November 21, 1977, with enforcement to begin on May 3, 1978. Permanent program regulations were scheduled for completion by August 3, 1978. To provide for any necessary, viable changes, the OSM was mandated to hold public hearings and to allow a thirty-day comment period from interested parties and state governments.

States desiring primary regulatory authority (primacy) were required to submit, by January 31, 1979, proposals that met the standards of the act and the federal permanent program. Following a review of the primacy proposal and an examination of public hearing transcripts, the OSM would approve or deny the state's proposal. If primacy was denied, the state was given sixty days to submit a revised proposal. The OSM would continue as primary authority in cases where a state failed to submit or to receive approval of its primacy application.

The act confronts the environmental degradation of past mining abuses by requiring mining companies to deposit a reclamation fee into an Abandoned Mine Reclamation Fund. The fees varied depending on the company's annual production rate, the type of coal mined, and the mining technique being used. As an incentive, states receiving primacy would receive a portion of this fund to aid in restoring unreclaimed mine sites.

Additionally, the act establishes 114 detailed mining and reclamation performance standards for the industry. Examples—required in the interim, permanent and approved state programs—require mine operators to (1) submit detailed information on the proposed mine site and a reclamation plan before a permit to mine is issued; (2) secure a performance bond of sufficient size to pay for reclamation should the mine operator fail to do so; (3) remove and store topsoil separately so it can be used in reclamation; (4) conduct blasting only under specified conditions; (5) monitor and take steps to ensure that mining does not adversely affect the water quality or hydrological balance of the mined area; (6) handle and store spoil materials only in specified ways, with no placement of spoil on the downslope; (7) reclaim portions of the mined area as quickly as possible after mining is completed; (8) eliminate all highwalls in the reclamation process; (9) regrade the mined area to its approximate original contour; and (10) establish a self-revegetating cover on the mined area. Other sections of the act include provisions designed to restrict coal mining in certain ecologically fragile or economically significant areas, such as prime farmlands and alluvial valley floors in the West.

Generally the act's requirements are comprehensive and stringent, containing many "agency forcing" provisions (cf. Ackerman and Hassler, 1981). For example, a mandatory system of inspection and enforcement is included along with procedures for the assessment and collection of civil penalties levied against coal companies who violate the OSM's regulations. However, this stringency and rigidity are deceptive. By including procedures for variances from the act's requirements, Congress left to the OSM the task of resolving issues related to the breadth and application of several performance standards. More importantly, the relationship between the new agency and state regulatory authorities was left ambiguous. The OSM's task is to ensure that the states develop adequate regulatory programs, but responsibility for long-range development and implementation was left to the states. Thus, the act contains the seeds for serious tension and conflict. In subsequent chapters, we examine this conflict and document its impact on the OSM's efforts to implement the new law.

# 4 The Social Construction of the Agency

The efficacy of law is largely a product of administration. Well before its passage, President Carter's new Secretary of the Interior, Cecil Andrus, created an interagency task force to prepare for implementation of the anticipated surface mining statute. Eventually, some ninety persons from approximately twenty agencies comprised the OSMRE Task Force. This task force was broken down into seventeen task groups, each of which worked on developing a piece of the new Office of Surface Mining and its regulatory programs. As the task force grew in size, an increasing amount of the work was delegated to the task groups.

The task force was destined to remain in place for longer than had been anticipated. The attachment of the controversial B-1 bomber bill to the surface mining act appropriations bill delayed funding for seven months. This delay exacerbated the normal difficulties of agency construction. Hiring of agency personnel was delayed. During the interim, the task force functioned as the proto-agency.

The appointed task force leader was a career civil servant who previously held a managerial position in the Department of the Interior. Like him, most members of the task force were recruited or specifically assigned from other agencies in the Department of Interior. Only a few had direct ties to the anti-strip mining or environmental movements. Most were selected for their technical expertise in mining or in related areas such as hydrology and geology. The OSM needed these technical experts to help draft its interim regulations and, later, to help review state primacy applications. Career civil servants (most were assigned only temporarily to the task) laid the administrative foundations of the Office of Surface Mining. However, the influence of a few activist reformers had a strong impact on the evolving organization.

## CONSTRUCTING LEGISLATIVE HISTORY

The final days of the legislative deliberations over the Surface Mining Act provided the task force with important tasks to perform. Task force members quietly cooperated with congressional staff to shape the OSM's enabling legislation:

> The first chore was the last minute lobbying. Were there things in this act which we wanted to change—now that it looked like it was going to be signed? So, we collected a series of possible adjustments. So, first we had to identify those. . . . So there was lobbying going on in the sense of the administration expressing its views and taking a position on some of the spicy issues: prime farmland, alluvial valley floors. While at the same time preparing a set of what might be called technical amendments.

In addition, task force leaders worked with Congress to craft a legislative history that would provide an unequivocal defense against the litigation anticipated after the promulgation of regulations:

> We got legislative history. We asked the committee to put in an extra sentence or two in the committee report. Or . . . we wrote floor colloquies, where you have Senator _____ saying, "Isn't it correct Congressman so-and-so that . . .?" (They're all made up you know. He's reading off a cue sheet.) But those are the last minute kind of mechanics of legislation. You'd see where you'd get a little mechanical weakness in the way a statute would work, and if that fell apart, you'd have this enormous discontinuity and screw up. And the mechanical hook . . . can be strengthened by just the right kind of legislative history. . . . And you can tighten that so it's closed with a nice sentence or two, or colloquy. Or, better yet, something in the committee report.

To avoid becoming entangled in the final stages of the legislative battle over the act, the task force operated unobtrusively in writing the interim regulations:

> One of the things we attempted—and, I think, reasonably adequately—was to keep task force operations out of the debate and

hearings and markups going on the Hill. Now, there were two or three of us who were working with the secretary's legislative people, and what he wanted to do on the Hill. And we'd point out some of the problems we had. But as far as the run-of-the-mill task force, you know, the people who were actually trying to develop the agency infrastructure, we just, as much as we could, we severed that. And we were very careful, or tried to be very careful, that the draft regulations didn't get out into industry, or up on the Hill, floating around.

## CONSTRUCTING THE ORGANIZATION

The task force selected an organizational structure having five regional offices for the Office of Surface Mining. This structure permitted a substantial degree of decentralization. It also allowed the development of regional programs that could be, to some extent, tailored to the varying conditions and demands of different areas of the country. Finally, it promoted a degree of timely responsiveness, which would be difficult if most problem solving and decisions were handled at headquarters. Consequently, in opting for this type of organizational structure, the task force recognized some need for regional autonomy. In addition, the physical separation of the regional offices from the central offices of the various state programs symbolized the new agency's independence.

The OSM located its five regional offices in Charleston, West Virginia; Knoxville, Tennessee; Indianapolis, Indiana; Kansas City, Missouri; and Denver, Colorado. The formal structure of the regional offices paralleled the structure of headquarters. The location and geographical coverage of the respective regions is depicted in Figure 4-1.

Due to OSM's resource delays, its initial representatives in some of the coal fields were attorneys from the Solicitor's Office. Several regional directors reported to work to find the initial group of inspectors already working under the direction of task force leaders and these regional solicitors. These reform-minded attorneys initiated the enforced compliance style that was to characterize most of the evolving regional programs. By early 1978, the essential direction of the OSM's regulatory programs had been determined. By the time headquarters executives and their regional counterparts took their posts, an enforced compliance interpretation of the agency's mission already had found wide acceptance in the Office of Surface Mining.

Because of congressional delays in appropriations, the agency's director could not be hired until several months after the effective date of the act. A professional engineer, he formerly served as head of surface mining regulation in Pennsylvania, the state touted for its exemplary pre-1977

Figure 4-1
OSM Regions

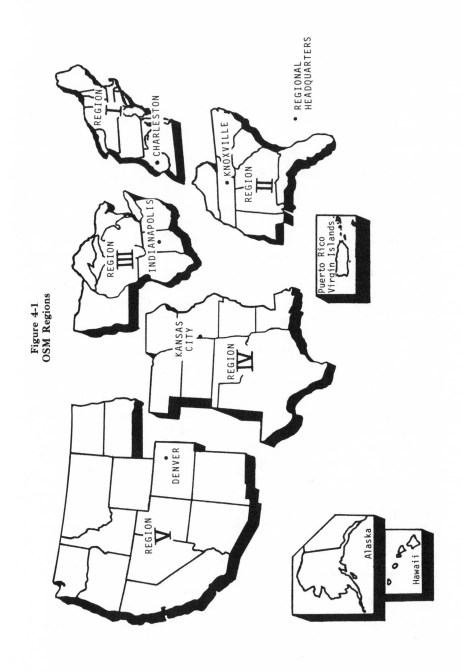

REGION I
CHARLESTON

REGION II
KNOXVILLE

REGION III
INDIANAPOLIS

REGION IV
KANSAS CITY

REGION V
DENVER

Puerto Rico
Virgin Islands

Alaska
Hawaii

• REGIONAL
  HEADQUARTERS

regulatory program. During the legislative battles, he was one of a handful of state regulators who testified in favor of federal legislation. Thus, his selection was acceptable both to the states and the environmentalist community. Like the new director, the agency's initial assistant directors were not hired until mid-1978, several months after creation of the task force.[1]

## CONSTRAINING FACTORS

The task force worked under four broad constraints on its definition of mission, policy, and regulations: (1) its perception of a mandate for a stringent surface mining program, (2) its guiding ideology, (3) the differential organization and effectiveness of external groups, and (4) statutory time restrictions.

### The Perceived Mandate

When he signed the SMCRA in the White House rose garden, President Carter publicly expressed his disappointment that the bill was not as "tough" as he would have liked. The president's openly-expressed sympathies for environmental protection and his appointment of several persons with similar leanings to important positions in the Department of the Interior combined to send a symbolic message to members of the task force. They believed that the Carter administration wanted a regulatory program that would strongly favor environmental protection rather than developmentalism. They perceived a similar congressional mandate because surface mining legislation had been passed twice. In the words of a task force member, belief in mandate stringency was "in the air on the sixth floor of the Interior Building" as the interim program took shape.

Little concern for *developmentalism* (economic growth) was apparent at the time. Although economic stagnation nationally had begun to take its toll on social regulatory programs, the task force was unaffected by these developments. As they began to work, the coal industry was enjoying prosperous times. In 1977–1978 coal production and prices stood at all-time highs. Although profits had declined from their peak in the early years of OPEC, they remained high by historic standards (U.S. Department of Labor, 1981:27,55,57). It seemed reasonable to presume that the coal industry easily could absorb or pass along to its customers the costs of regulation.

## The Guiding Ideology

Although most task force personnel were selected for their technical expertise, some of its members sought positions because they welcomed the opportunity to shape a program to correct strip mining abuses. A solicitor told us that the OSM "attracted a large portion of people who were extremely enthusiastic about the goals of [the] statute." Such persons brought to their work both commitment and a sense of mission. An important task force member told us, "We were reformers." Asked if he meant everyone on the task force, he replied, "Everyone who counted."[2]

Consequently, several members of the task force were distrustful of the coal industry's motives. They had observed nearly a decade of the industry's congressional testimony that they believed to be untrue or extremely misleading. Further, they attributed the history of lax state regulation to the machinations of the coal industry. They fully expected the coal industry to challenge and fight the new agency and its regulatory program at every opportunity and in every forum. Anticipating conflict, task force leaders became concerned with designing a program that could withstand legal challenge. This desire for defensibility thrust the agency's attorneys into a prominent role in drafting regulations and shaping the program. These attorneys were assigned to the OSM by the Department of Interior's Solicitor's Office.

Functioning in the context of critical external scrutiny, resource delays, and agency construction under the crisis conditions of rigorous deadlines, the solicitors enjoyed several advantages. Because it is funded separately, the Solicitor's Office already had an operating budget and a full complement of personnel. The Solicitor's Office did not operate with temporary personnel loaned from other agencies. The solicitors were "on the ground and running," and they played an active, major part in creating the OSM's regulatory programs. Important decisions were deferred to them, as an influential task force member noted:

> There's a tendency in federal government—and we were no different—to, rather than go to the attorney and say, "this is what I *want* to do," to go to the attorney and say, "what *can* I do?" So, [the influence of the attorneys] was a function of, you know, the tendency to ask rather than tell what you wanted to do, I guess.

Among the major program consequences were the reinforcement of an adversarial mode of dealing with some of their constituencies and an emphasis on detail and precision in the regulations. There was considerably less discussion of whether the regulations were reasonable.

Some influential members of the task force viewed with skepticism the states' willingness to implement strong regulatory programs. They assumed that the states would drag their feet or, worse, would actively resist the OSM's efforts to prod them into a more effective regulatory posture. A solicitor noted, "I think there was a healthy skepticism about the willingness of the states to change direction." Consequently, when states later began to object to OSM decisions, the new federal regulators did not take them seriously. The same respondent told us:

> I *suppose* that the resistance of the state institutions was somewhat discounted [by OSM], on the rationale that "well, the whole purpose of the Act was to change these people, and they're not gonna like it anyway. *Discount* it."

Eventually, the OSM's developing enforced compliance style left the agency vulnerable to charges by industry and the states that it was arrogant and unwilling to listen to parties with alternative views on regulation.

### Differential Effectiveness of External Groups

During the legislative struggle, the coal industry's opposition was adamant and cavalier. It developed few new organizational arrangements to defeat legislation, relying instead on sympathetic members of Congress and Republican presidents to stall the regulatory movement. When the act passed, the coal industry determined to fight harder for its own brand of regulation. Larger mining companies created a Joint Committee of the National Coal Association (NCA) and the American Mining Congress (AMC) to represent their interests. Smaller mining companies established the Washington-based Mining and Reclamation Council of America (MARC).

Unlike the coal industry, citizens and environmentalists already had in place a disciplined and responsive national coalition. When the task force began its work, this national coalition worked very effectively to shape the emerging program. An important member of the task force told us:

> The environmentalists were more constant in being in, in asking for meetings, looking at what's going on. And that [was] true all the way, all the way through. My experience with OSM is that you had—and it varied with individuals—but, an individual from an

environmental organization, once you met him he was likely to be in fairly regular.

Importantly, the national environmentalists' coalition was one of the only dependable sources of support for the new Office of Surface Mining. Stated simply, few if any other constituencies clearly desired a federal regulatory presence. The fact that several members of the task force shared the environmentalists' reformist orientation served only to cement the natural affinity between the two groups. This bond, together with the organizational effectiveness of the environmentalist movement, generated a measure of mutual respect and deference.

In contrast to the environmentalists, a key member of the task force told us that the coal

> industry was more spotty, with few exceptions. . . . There was a different approach. You could tell a difference. And that probably had an influence. I'd say the constant contact of environmentalists [had an influence]. But, again, I don't think anyone was ever told "no, I can't meet with you," to my knowledge.

Representatives of the coal industry received a formally correct and polite reception from the task force. An industry spokesman said:

> You have to believe that there was an intent not to have contact. I don't know how you could believe anything else. I mean, the results of three-and-a-half years of constant efforts of one side and nothing on the other side has to lead you to believe that there was no desire to have contact.

Although he clearly is unaccustomed to this kind of treatment from federal regulators, the same subject acknowledged that

> I could generally get through to them, yeah. I'd be delayed a lot of times, but we had contact with them. Don't get me wrong, we had contact with them. But it was always initiated from our side. No one ever told you, "Well, look, something big is coming up. Get ready for it." The only way you ever—let me characterize the communications. Communication was: We go down and we talk with them, and we see our answer in the *Federal Register*. Okay? That's how we get an answer, the *Federal Register*.

Our data suggest that the respondent did not exaggerate. A task force member told us:

> I will say the environmentalists—and bless them, there's some great ones—were so delighted over their offspring that they paid a lot of attention to it in the early days. It was . . . like they had produced this beautiful child, and they couldn't quite leave it alone. . . . [The OSM] had too much "loving care" from the environmentalists.

In short order, the sympathetic hearing afforded environmentalists infuriated the coal industry, which now added to its growing list of complaints the charge that the agency was staffed with "environmental zealots."

## Statutory Time Restrictions

Fully aware that regulatory bureaucracies may become excessively accommodative toward regulated firms, framers of the Surface Mining Act sought to avert these tendencies. They did so in large part by binding the OSM to a detailed, rigorous implementation schedule. As noted, the SMCRA required the new agency to develop, within ninety days after enactment of the law, an interim regulatory program for all surface coal mining operations. Then, within one year of enactment, the OSM was to publish its permanent program regulations.

Congressional leaders worried that these deadlines were too restrictive. Eager to get on with the job, newly appointed Interior officials assured Congress that the implementation schedule could be met. Certainly, the new Department of Interior leadership was not very prescient. As it turned out, the need to meet mandated deadlines was a major constraint on the agency's operations during its first three years.[3]

The interim regulations were written under the intense pressure of a mandated deadline. What should have been a studied, methodical process was truncated severely. The task force could not subject its procedures and proposals to the critical internal debate that often leads to the detection and correction of mistakes and potential problems. Since time did not permit an extended assessment of relevant options, they concentrated on getting the job done (i.e., constructing the regulations quickly). An important member of the task force noted this problem:

> It would have been useful to have [records of options considered]. It'd be useful for things like you guys are doing, to go back and

see what was considered. Some parts of the program went through more debate than others, you know. There were some pretty hard debates about the enforcement program, and I think three or four options that were documented fairly heavily. It wasn't so much an effort to try to sit down and try to write out your options as it was, "Well, let's develop this one and see where it leads, develop this one and see where it leads, develop this one" type of thing. It was less formal. Had to be.

Although the complex and technical nature of their mandate lent itself well to an open, collegial management style, time constraints led the task force to choose a hierarchical, centralized method of operation instead. Imposition of severe hierarchical dynamics on top of a work process that limited debate and questioning undermined further the task force's ability to weigh the practical consequences of their actions. Effectively, the process of writing regulations was influenced disproportionately by a small number of task force members: (1) those with or without formal authority who acquired power because of their ability to "get things done," and (2) those who understood the arcane ways and requirements of the federal bureaucracy and used this knowledge to achieve task force objectives.

## IMPLICATIONS

From its origins in the task force, the OSM was constructed by state managers. They saw their task as the rationalization of an industry that was out of control in causing environmental damage. The Surface Mining Act was written in full recognition of capture theory of regulation. Subsequently, the coal industry was almost completely isolated from the agency construction process. The spirit of the environmentalist movement was well represented in the new agency. But it cannot be said that the OSM was an instrument of that movement. Rather, the managers of OSM were responsive to the political and economic context of the times. The environmentalist movement was still a strong political force in Congress and in the Carter administration. The economy, especially the coal industry, was not facing an accumulation crisis. The state managers acted to legitimate the role of the state as governor of capital. In so acting, they appealed to the law itself for their mandate and founded an agency that, from its roots, stressed an enforced compliance approach to regulation. However, the ambiguity of the law concerning state-federal relations necessarily was reflected in the organization of the OSM. The agency was structured to remain separate from capture by the states as well as the coal industry. The loose organizational coupling between the agency and the various state programs was incompatible with a strict enforced compliance strategy. The decision to pursue an enforced compliance style in the rule-making process exacerbated existing tensions between the agency and the states.

# 5 The Social Construction of Regulations

Social scientists have conducted a great deal of research on the law-making process. Most of their attention has focused on statutes and case law; however, previous investigators have largely ignored the promulgtion of regulatory law. We contend that making regulatory law involves the same political mechanisms as these other law-making processes. Once a law is passed, the conflict between interest groups involved in the formulation of the statute shifts to the rule making. Procedures require formal communication through open public hearings and publicly available comments. However, this public comment period occurs after the regulations have been drafted by a select group of technicians and bureaucrats. Consequently, the initial construction of regulations occurs outside these structured procedures. Because regulations must be crafted more meticulously than the statutes from which they are derived, attorneys and technical specialists become the key players in the drafting of regulations. At this early stage, communications are analogous to legislative lobbying. Typically, informal communication networks during the drafting have greater influence over the finished product than do the later public hearings or comments. Thus, rule making remains a political process of conflict and negotiation between interested parties, but it is removed from the hands of elected politicians and from the glare of public scrutiny. Such was the case in the development of federal surface mining regulations.

While creating regulations, technicians and bureaucrats make political decisions. The choice between promulgating design standards or performance standards is a case in point. Having determined the regulatory standard it wants firms to meet, a regulatory agency has two options: it can emphasize use of *design standards* or *performance standards.* If it opts for the latter, the agency requires firms to meet specific standards in the production process (e.g., maximum permissible amount of sediment in water flowing from a mine site), but leaves to the firm's discretion how to meet the standard. If it opts for the former, the agency requires that firms meet specific performance standards and use specific technologies in doing so (e.g., control sediment runoff by constructing sedimentation ponds).

## THE POLITICAL CONTEXT

The Office of Surface Mining received its mandate and began operations amidst continuing rancorous political conflict. Now, the bitter legislative adversaries turned their attention to the Office of Surface Mining and its rule-making process. Each wanted and expected to have a significant part in shaping the forthcoming regulations.

An attorney who represents environmentalist and citizens' groups noted the difficulties this portended for the agency:

> Strip mining, in my mind, has been one of the most controversial areas in the entire realm of federal regulations. . . . Now, why has it been so controversial? . . . It was terribly contested in Congress. . . . [I]t was bitterly contested. . . . Therefore, I think anyone who thought that it was going to be implemented without a great deal of problems was just whistling into the wind. There were bound to be problems—if the agency stuck to its mandate—'cause, simply put, a number of the major coal states and coal operators never accepted the Surface Mining Act, when it was on the Hill or when it was passed.

Although the SMCRA is a detailed enabling statute, with numerous agency-forcing provisions, the OSM retained considerable discretion and latitude in defining its mission and corresponding policies. As the agency began the rule-making process, its executives expected the coal industry to resist their efforts, both in litigation and also on Captiol Hill. They expected the states to drag their feet or balk at federal efforts to strengthen their regulatory programs.

## THE OSM'S RULE-MAKING PROCESS

Leaders in the Department of Interior and in the Office of Surface Mining wanted the new regulations to be an exemplary product. To the professional state managers, this meant simply creating the Office of Surface Mining and meeting its statutory deadlines. Not only would this please the new leadership in the Department of Interior, but it also would serve as undeniable evidence of substantial leadership and organizational abilities.

The need to move quickly to promulgate regulations led OSM's headquarters executives to maintain the highly centralized management style of task force days. This strategy enabled them to keep a close rein on the regulation production process. Short of time already, they were unable to draw upon regional staff for assistance or for critical feedback while producing the agency's regulations. The regions understood why they were excluded, but they noted it just the same:

> Some of the folks at headquarters were not "field oriented." Of course, they were giving their full time to regulation writing. That was driving headquarters. . . . They were doing it pretty much in a vacuum. . . . The regional directors . . . were never consulted. The regional directors had no input into the regulations. . . . we were so preoccupied with implementing the interim program, and hiring people, [and opening field offices].

Expecting the coal industry to resist regulation, headquarters managers were virtually obsessed by the desire to ensure that everything connected with the promulgation process was done correctly. The agency's leadership was dependent on the personnel and resources at hand. They desperately needed committed and capable individuals to help complete its mandated tasks. Consequently, they came to rely upon employees who quickly proved themselves capable of delivering a quality work product on a very tight schedule. Employees who worked long hours and were productive necessarily acquired influence in the process. This description fits most of the Office of Surface Mining's original employees, most particularly the solicitors.

The agency needed its solicitors' expertise if it hoped to avoid major appellate damage to the regulatory program. This solidified the solicitors' increasingly prominent role in constructing the agency and shaping its mission and policies. Moreover, the solicitors' eagerness and commitment were whetted by early skirmishes over the agency and its regulations.

> Q: What was the effect, for individuals and for groups of people working together, of being under continuous attack?
> A: Well, as far as the lawyers—the people in the Solicitor's Office— were concerned, many of us had come from litigation backgrounds

and were very used to that kind of situation. So, it really just fueled our fires all the more, I think.

The solicitors and the OSM's leadership held the same objectives for the agency. They wanted to win the important court battles that were certain to come. Victory there would vindicate them and serve as an enduring reminder of their legal and bureaucratic skills. They would present industry with no opportunities to undo their regulatory handiwork. The solicitors were determined that the agency's rule-making process would be flawless.

The lawyers' new centrality and power intensified antagonisms for them within the OSM, especially with the agency's technical personnel.

> [The lawyers] were probably the most hated of the whole group. The agency hated them because the lawyers would say: "No, this is inadequate, insufficient. You haven't interpreted the law right"— whatever. Made . . . [the regulations] harder, made them do it [over]. . . . [A] huge animosity developed between lawyers and the agency. And then, you know, [agency personnel would say]: "Whose policy call is it, anyway? . . . And who's developing this program?" So, all that friction. And the lawyers felt the agency people were dumb and, you know, dim witted.

The solicitors believed that OSM's technical personnel did not appreciate the importance and perils of the agency's rule-making process. They criticized the technical staff for failure to prepare thorough and detailed technical support for draft regulations.

> [F]or every one OSM hour, you had about five lawyer hours on top of that. Patching, correcting, writing. . . . [T]he lawyers really took an incredibly poor work product and made it what . . . held up in court. . . . [Those] folks worked extraordinarily hard.

When the agency promulgated its permanent regulations, a majority of the small group that wrote them were attorneys.

## FEDERAL SURFACE MINING REGULATIONS

Federal law requires that the Office of Surface Mining follow specific procedures in promulgating its regulations. First, the agency must publish proposed rules (i.e., draft regulations) in the *Federal Register.* It then must hold public hearings on the proposed regulations and request written comments as well. Commenters are asked to provide supporting materials and technical data to sustain their comments and suggested revisions. These materials and transcripts of public hearings of the proposed rules are placed in the agency's administrative record for public inspection. Personal contacts between agency personnel and parties to the developing regultory program must be carefully monitored or banned entirely. After the public comment period officially closes, agency personnel meet to weigh the comments and to craft their final regulations. In a preamble to the final regulations, the agency responds to each comment it receives on the proposed regulations and provides a brief rationale for rejecting alternative versions of the regulations.

Between September 7, 1977, and March 13, 1979, the Office of Surface Mining published four sets of surface coal mining regulations: proposed interim regulations (*Federal Register* 42 [7 September 1977]: 44920–57); final interim regulations *(Federal Relgister* 42 [13 December 1977]: 62639–713); proposed permanent regulations *(Federal Register* 43 [18 September 1978]: 41661–940); and final permanent regulations *Federal Register* 44 [13 March 1979]: 14901–15463).

These four sets of regulations serve as important and revealing indicators of the OSM's fundamental approach to its regulatory task. To focus our efforts and also to economize on project resources, we examined a sample of regulations for clues to OSM's regulatory biases. The four issues we examined intensively were not selected at random from OSM's nearly 700 regulations. Rather, we selected issues that were controversial in specific regions of the United States or for only segments of the coal industry. For analytical purposes, we assumed that the four sets of regulations represent an underlying linear develomental process. We tried to approximate "an ethnography of rule-making" (Shapiro, 1980:37) by drawing both from interviews anb analyses of written materials.

To examine the relative effectiveness of contending parties in the rule-making process, we reviewed the OSM's administrative record of comments and materials submitted by citizens and groups. Changes in the wording of regulations are the outcome of political struggle in the rule-making process. Consequently, we noted changes in the regulations and linked them to the objectives sought and comments submitted by the various groups.

## Sedimentation Ponds

Surface coal mining in the East causes severe ecological damage to streams due to acid mine drainage and soil erosion. In the words of an environmentalist lawyer, "Sediment is *the* major problem associated with strip mining." Public Law 95–87 addressed the sedimentation problem by requiring mining firms "to prevent, to the extent possible using the best technology currently available, additional contributions of suspended solids to streamflow, or runoff outside the permit area," to construct "siltation structures" prior to mining, "as certified by qualified registered engineer," and to remove settling ponds after reclamation (section 515. [b] [10] [B] [ii]).

The phrase "best technology currently available" was used by the rule-making task force as rationale for stringent sedimentation pond design criteria.[1] The proposed interim rules stated that settling ponds shall be constructed at all mining sites (section 715.123. [e]).[2] The sedimentation pond requirement was defended by OSM as the "state of the art" in sedimentation control. The original proposed design criteria specified that storage volume of ponds must include 0.2 acre-feet for each acre of disturbed land additional capacity to handle a ten-year, twenty-four-hour precipitation event. These design criteria exceeded the standards of states with sedimentation pond regulations.

As a measure to control sediment runoff, the coal industry would have preferred a simple performance standard for suspended solids in streams and mine site runoff. The rules for the construction of sedimentation ponds were immediately attacked by industry, and some states and the OSM encountered strong pressure for revision. This pressure came directly from some of the states and from industry trade associations. For example, the West Virginia Surface Mining and Reclamation Association concluded its comments with an appeal:

> West Virginia has a proven drainage control program offering many solutions to operational problems. Why not adopt a proven program that is superior to a one shot solution that may or may not work. [C27][3]

A Pennsylvania coal association estimated that the federal rules would require storage capacity eight times as large and eight times as costly as current state practice.

Numerous comments by the coal industry on the sedimentation pond regulations can be boiled down to one major complaint: compliance with pond design criteria necessarily would result in extremely large ponds. Constructing these ponds in mountainous areas would be extremely difficult and very costly. The outcry came from the eastern coal industry, both large and small, and from eastern states. Small operators especially were incensed because they would pay a higher cost per ton of coal for pond construction.

The industry's *cri de coeur* against design standards is represented in a state coal association recommendation

> that engineers be given a choice between set "cookbook" criteria and utilizing best engineering principles to arrive at an end result compatible with the intent of the Act. Site specific criteria must be met. [F-381]

Environmentalists generally supported the OSM's decisions to require use of sedimentation ponds and to specify stringent pond design criteria. They hoped that operators simply would not mine areas where the requisite ponds could not be constructed and maintained properly. But they knew coal operators too well to think that this would happen. Once it became clear that sedimentation ponds constructed in compliance with the agency's design criteria would be very large, they tempered somewhat their support for the original pond regulations. Less than three years before, the collapse of an earthen mining dam had killed 125 persons and wiped out several communities in Buffalo Creek, West Virginia (Erikson, 1976). Environmentalists were reluctant to support vigorously regulations that could increase the chances of similar tragedies in the future. They were similarly worried about the potential hazard posed by building multiple levels of sedimentation ponds in steep Appalachian hollows. They were also concerned about the environmental damage that would result simply in the process of constructing sedimentation ponds.

In response to industry's comments, OSM's final interim regulation recognized alternative "sediment control measures." Nonetheless, the pond requirement was retained. Despite complaints by industry, the regulation added further design criteria: a twenty-four-hour detention time and a surface area of one square foot for each fifty gallons per day of inflow resulting from the design standard precipitation event.

The coal industry sought relief in the courts; the OSM withdrew and revised the regulation. Now credits would be given so that the required 0.2 acre-feet of storage volume could be reduced. In addition, the twenty-four-hour detention time criterion could be reduced to ten hours if the operator demonstrated adequate supplementary control measures. Finally, the surface area per inflow criterion was dropped. These revisions were effective immediately, prior to a public comment period, in order "to provide immediate guidance to State regulatory agencies and coal operators." The revisions did not satisfy the coal industry.

The final interim and permanent program regulations are essentially identical.[4] However, additional justification for the sedimentation pond requirement in the permanent program was based on technical studies conducted by the Environmental Protection Agency. The coal industry was given further relief on one major design criterion, the 0.2 acre-feet storage volume standard.[5] It was reduced to 0.1 acre-feet with possible reduction to 0.035 acre-feet if the operator utilizes additional erosion and sedimentation control measures. These standards were suggested by a major coal association in the first round of comments, and they were supported by eastern states with strong reclamation programs. Essentially, the Office of Surface Mining admitted that the technical basis for its 0.2 acre-feet requirement had been weak.

In the struggle to establish primary design criteria for sedimentation ponds, the coal industry clearly prevailed on some issues. But they were hardly satisfied. In the words of one industry representative:

> The changes in regulations . . . are somewhat analogous to the housepainter with a 20 foot ladder who has been assigned to paint the top of a 60 foot flagpole. Upon recognizing his error in assignments, the foreman assigns the painter another job—a 40 foot flagpole. [U.S. Congress, House, 1979:487]

The coal industry was less influential than the Environmental Protection Agency and environmentalists in establishing the basic rules for sedimentation control. The final standards probably were more stringent than those of any state program. The ten-hour detention period, the result of a previous compromise in industry's favor, was not changed even though it was still opposed. Sedimentation ponds were still required and industry's call to eliminate an array of specific design standards in favor of turning everything over to professional engineers was rejected. In other instances as well, the coal industry clearly lost ground in the permanent rules. For example, the proposed interim rules had required pond cleaning when sediment had accumulated to 50 percent of the required storage volume. This number was first modified to 80 percent, then eliminated altogether, only to reappear as 60 percent in the final rules.

The industry won some points on specific design standards, Nevertheless, the permanent program rules contain many more requirements than the interim regulations.

## Permissible Variation in State Programs

State surface mining regulators and elected officials believed that local geographical and climatological conditions necessitated regional regulatory variation. Their early experiences with OSM caused them to doubt the agency's willingness to permit this regulatory diversity. Although relationships between the task force and the states were good in the early months of the former's operations, these amicable relations gradually began to deteriorate. They gradually became disenchanted with OSM and its headquarters executives.

As an OSM headquarters executive noted, the section of the regulations known as the "state window" took shape in this context:

> [W]e found . . . that the states were saying, "You're inflexible, rigid; you won't allow differences." We'd been saying all along, without effect, that, "We are flexible; we will allow differences." And the states said, "Well, show us in these regulations where it says that." It didn't say that. We had started the whole process with the idea in our minds that we were flexible, that there was a lot of room, and that the words we had written into the [interim] regulations would allow the states to do things quite differently. And we never stopped and looked back to see whether it was clear to the states. . . . As a result . . . we found ourselves being hammered by states and others for our rigidity and inflexibility. The state window was our solution to this. And in our minds . . . this was to make clear what we had already intended.

The OSM decided to add a section to the new regulations wherein they would signal a willingness to be flexible. The resulting state window provisions appeared for the first time in the OSM's proposed permanent regulations. As contained in section 731.13, the state window provided that states could request approval from OSM for alternative regulatory standards and procedures in the areas of permitting, bonding, inspection, enforcement, and the performance standards in the act. When requesting approval, a state was required to describe the alternative approach, provide statutory or regulatory language that would be used to implement it, and explain and present data to show that the alternative approach would be consistent with the act and would "achieve the same or more stringent regulatory results."[6]

The coal industry supported the state window concept. For example, the notes from a November meeting between members of the NCA-AMC Joint Committee and OSM's assistant director for state and federal programs indicates that the "Joint committee favors inclusion of State window" (F-461). However, industry commenters pressed for amendments to the state window provision that would permit the states even greater latitude in program development. Island Creek Coal Company sounded a typical industry theme: "We accept the statement . . . that no leeway be permitted in achieving the *results* specified in the Act; but we object to the [OSM] restraints on *alternative methods* of achieving those results" (F-470; emphasis in original). In a word, the coal industry favored the concept of specific criteria for approval of state regulatory programs, but argued that the state window criteria were too inflexible. They were supported on this point by the states themselves. In fact the debate over the state window nurtured a developing coalition between the coal industry and the states, in opposition to the environmentalists and what they perceived as the high-handedness of the Office of Surface Mining.

On October 4, 1978, OSM's headquarters executives met with regulatory officials from six states who were representing the Interstate Mining Compact Commission. The state representatives inquired of OSM, "What recourse does a State have if its alternative submissions are turned down?" They went on to suggest deletion of several words— "the same or more stringent than"—from the state window provision (F-17). In written comments submitted several weeks later, the IMCC suggested language changes for section 731.13, which would grant approval to state programs containing regulatory requirements "*capable of achieving* the same or more stringent . . . results" (F-58).

In a similar vein, on November 9, 1979, OSM headquarters executives and Region V managers met in Denver with representatives of six western states. Regarding the state window, the meeting minutes indicate the

> [g]eneral reaction of the States was that the regulations should be stated more in the form of general goals which the States should meet. Less specificity should be given, and the State window should be broadened to provide that any provisions which would meet the general goals could be accepted. [The states] expressed particular concern regarding the definition of the phrase "consistent with" and of the way the phrase is used. . . . The definition of "consistent with" to mean "the same as or similar to" appears to run contrary to the State window concept. . . . The States expressed the belief that this makes the State window meaningless. [F-166].

As these comments suggest, inclusion of the state window in OSM's proposed permanent regulations did little to mollify the states. In a

November 17, 1978, letter to OSM's director, Tennessee's commissioner of conservation charged that the proposed permanent regulations

> reflect the attitude OSM has consistently demonstrated regarding federal-state relationships during the development of the interim program and, thus far, during the development of the permanent program—an attitude and a policy position which Tennessee finds highly objectionalbe. . . . [A] review of the agency's proposed draft reveals voluminous, unnecessary, duplicative red tape and bureaucratic limitations that are designed to take this program away from the states, directly ignoring the intent of Congress. . . . Our recommendations are for extensive revision to the proposed regulations in order to provide the states necessary management flexibility required to respond to the diversity of mining conditions and to create the state-federal partnership necessary to achieve the results specified in the Act. [F-551]

The objectives sought by industry and the states in the state window provision were precisely those the environmentalist groups found most objectionable. Whereas the former parties wanted to open wide the state window, the latter groups feared such a move because of what the opened window might admit. In a meeting on October 26, 1978, with an OSM executive, lawyers representing the Council of the Southern Mountains expressed a concern that "the state window approach was too broad and was not thought out" (F-209). The same opinions were expressed by the same attorneys—this time accompanied by a representative of the National Wildlife Federation, in a November 29, 1978, meeting with OSM's director, an assistant director, and a representative of the Solicitor's Office (F-449). On November 27, 1978, the director of the Environmental Policy Center met with OSM's director and "questioned the need for the so called 'State Window'" (F-562). The Public Lands Institute suggested that the state window should be stricken entirely from the regulations since Congress intended "deviations from the Act and regulations can only be for greater stringency or more extensive coverage, but not for 'alternatives' which are in effect variances" (Letter, 17 November 1978).

As promulgated in final form on March 13, 1979, the state window, though retained, had been made considerably more difficult for the states to open.[7] The states continued to believe that the state window was too restrictive. Although it would be difficult to read this regulation as a clear victory for any party in the conflict, the states and the coal industry viewed it as a defeat.

## Alluvial Valley Floors

Whereas abundant rainfall creates the most severe environmental threats posed by surface mining in Appalachia, the problems are different in the West, where paucity of rainfall and ground water pose the most severe threats. If farming and ranching are to survive in the West, the quantity and distribution of fragile ground water supplies must be preserved. Preventing damage to these alluvial valley floors is essential to the preservation and distribution of ground water supplies.

An *alluvial valley floor* is an area in an otherwise arid region that is naturally irrigated or subirrigated to a degree sufficient to serve agricultural purposes. It is an area that is underlain with an acquifer. The Surface Mining Control and Reclamation Act mandates special environmental protection provisions for various regions of the country, including alluvial valley floors. Section 510.(b)(5) of the act provides that any proposed surface coal mining operation, if located west of the one hundredth meridian west longitude, must not "interrupt, discontinue, or preclude farming . . . on said valley floors" and must "not materially damage the quantity or quality of water in surface or underground water systems that supply" them. In section 715.17.9j) of the proposed interim regulations, OSM operationalized this section of the statute.[8]

The regulation imposes special obligations on surface miners in sections of the West to preserve the "essential elements of the hydrologic functions of alluvial valley floors throughout the mining and reclamation process." Surface mining and reclamation operations conducted in or adjacent to alluvial valley floors "shall not interrupt, discontinue, or preclude farming" in the mined areas. Except for certain grandfathered mines, future permit applicants were required to submit a variety of survey and baseline data used by the regulatory authority to assess the impact of mining operations on the area's specified hydrologic functions.

On one side, the coal industry pressed for regulations with narrow application and sought to increase regulatory flexibility (i.e., operators' range of discretion). For example, in their comments on the proposed interim regulations, the Joint Committee suggested that mine operators should be required to preserve the hydrologic functions of alluvial valley floors only "where necessary" (C83). Industry pleaded that restrictions on mining should be balanced against an assessment of the area's productive importance. Behind this plea was the fear that restrictions on mining on alluvial valley floors could jeopardize its large western coal leases.

On the other side, citizens' and environmentalist groups pushed for wide reaching regulations that would leave little discretion to coal operators or to the regulatory authority. Comments submitted by these groups urged the OSM to incorporate language from the act in the regulations and to increase the number of special regulatory requirements (C113; C257). For example, the Colorado Friends of the Earth requested an extension of regulatory protections to ground water that "effects alluvial valley floors" (C257).

The coal industry made few if any gains in the fight over the regulation of mining on alluvial floors. Successive versions of the OSM's regulations increased in length and detail. Changes in the regulation reflected the comments offered by citizens' groups. For example, section 715.17.(j)(2) of the proposed interim regulations stipulated that mining operations located in the arid West "shall not interrupt, discontinue, or preclude farming on . . . alluvial valley floors." The final interim regulation was revised before it was published as a final interim rule. The final regulation included a new stipulation: western mine operations "shall not materially damage the quantity or quality of surface ground water that supplies these valley floors.' Potentially, this extended the geographic coverage of the regulation to surface or ground water far from a self-contained mine site.

This one section of the regulations illustrates what appears to be a more general trend in the development of the OSM's regulations for alluvial valley floors. In fact, simple measurements of the number of *Federal Register* column inches devoted to regulation of alluvial valley floors in successive versions of the regulations may be a crude, but not misleading, indication of the overall nature of changes. In the proposed interim regulations, 8.25 column inches dealt with the issue (section 715.17.[j]). In the proposed permanent regulations, the amount of space increased to 74.75 column inches (sections 785.19; 786.17; 822) only to increase even more (to 81.92 inches) in the final permanent regulations (sections 785.19 and 822).[9]

## Citizen Participation in Inspection and Enforcement

Throughout the debate over surface mining regulation, provisions for citizen participation in surface mining regulation were urged on policy makers by environmentalists and opposed by the coal industry. Several regulations explicitly permit citizen participation. We selected one of them, citizen participation in inspection and enforcement, for analysis.

Section 721.13 of the proposed interim regulations permitted citizen participation in inspection and enforcement. It provided that any person who "suspects or knows" of a violation of the act or the regulations could request an inspection by OSM and some type of enforcement action. It guaranteed the citizen confidentiality unless electing to accompany the inspector, another right provided in the regulation. The regulation also required the OSM to inform the complainant of its findings within ten days of the inspection.[10]

The coal industry raised many objections to this regulation. The NCA-AMC Joint Committee argued:

> The provisions of the Act should not be triggered by a mere "Suspicion" but should require at least "reasonable belief" that a violation . . . has occurred. If the process is to be triggered by mere suspicion, then any disgruntled landowner seeking to negotiate a coal lease may invoke the onerous inspection and enforcement provisions of the Act as a bargaining tool to be used at his whim. [C83]

The committee suggested alternative language for the regulations that would delete the words "suspects or" from section 721.13.(a)(1). As rationale they indicated that "the danger of the agency being inundated with spurious 'suspicions' is compounded when the suspicious citizen is cloaked with anonymity" (C83). Echoing these comments and suggestions, the representative of a large mining corporation claimed that "there is no provision in the Act to authorize the Secretary to act on the basis of suspicion" (C34).

Industry commenters objected as well to the promise of complainant anonymity contained in the regulations. The president of a small mining company urged the deletion of section 721.13.(a)(2) in its entirety on the grounds that "it is a basic right of all Americans to know the identity of their accusor" (C159). Another industry representative indicated his strong objection

> to this attempt by OSM to create a secret police force of those individuals who, based upon some real or imagined danger to the environment or the public, have dedicated their lives to blocking any attempt by industry to provide energy to that public. [C276]

Industry representatives also pressed for specific clarification of who would be responsible for any injury to a citizen accompanying an OSM inspector onto a mine site. Some industry officials urged revision of the regulation so that, in the event of injury to the citizen complainant, "liability clearly lies with the Office of Surface Mining Reclamation and

Enforcement" (C34). Some commenters wished to go even further, indicating that the regulations should

> apply financial penalties to any citizen or organization who reports violations which require inspections where the reported violations are unsubstantiated. We expect both the cost of the Federal inspection and any losses in time or production incurred by the Operator to be borne by the person making the charges. [C145]

As the comments suggest, many representatives of mining companies seemed to fear that the citizen complaint provisions would encourage frivolous and harrassing complaints by vindictive citizens.

> You merely give the right to the Sierra Clubs, Old Ladies Auxiliary, etc. to harass any operating mine they wish to—and at the expense and with the help of the taxpayers—the U.S. Government. Strike this entire paragraph and procedure. [C26]

More importantly, several commenters suggested that the assurance of confidentiality provided complainants "appears to conflict with the open records requirements of the federal government" (C195).

A western coal producer challenged the regulation on grounds that citizens do not have legal standing:

> The proposed provision greatly enlarges citizen "standing" from [the Act] (" . . . any person who is or may be adversely affected . . .") to " . . . *any* person who *suspects* . . ." regardless of his interest in the violation. Such expanded citizen standing is without statutory authority. [C149; emphasis in original]

Fear of harassment by opponents of strip mining was the basic reason cited by industry to support their request that the regulations should not contain provisions protecting the confidentiality of informants. Industry argued that the draft regulation would permit extreme harassment of an operator by "disgruntled lessors, employees, landowners, creditors, customers, environmentalists, and/or any one in the general public who has an aversion to mining" (C130).

Advocates of strong citizens' rights provisions resisted industry's efforts to modify the regulations on citizen participation in inspection and enforcement:

[The provision] protecting the identity of the citizen reporting a suspected violation or known violations essential to allow the citizen report section to work. It has been heavily criticized by industry as violating the operator's sixth amendment right to be confronted by the witnesses against him and as serving no purpose for bona fide complaints. Neither of these has any rational basis. First, the witness against the operator would be the inspector, who, if a violation were found, would be confronting the operator. Secondly, many citizens would be reluctant to come forward if they would be, or fear they would be, harrassed, physically harmed, fired, or black listed. It is the lack of protection from reprisals that would keep a good citizen from filing a report, *not* the lack of a bona fide complaint. [C113; emphasis in original]

Environmentalist groups pressed for even stonger citizen's rights provisions. The primary reason for this stand was a fear that the federal and state regulatory agencies might be too accommodative toward the coal industry. Consequently, they sought to reduce or to eliminate all possible agency discretion in regulatory matters, especially in the area of inspection and enforcement.

Whereas industry grudgingly praised the requirement that citizen complaints to OSM about suspected regulatory violations be made *in writing*, environmentalist groups pressed for the recognition of *oral* complaints. An Appalachian citizens' group charged that

Sec. 721.13 is deficient in that it fails to allow any person to give oral notice to the [OSM] of violations. In a situation where an imminent danger is present the requirement of written notice may increase the liklihood of harm when time is of the essence. . . . If police agencies were to wait for written complaints of crimes in progress, it is likely that many offenders would escape detection. [C248]

The National Wildlife Federation made a similar proposal, suggesting that oral complaints could be "reduced to writing at some convenient time" (C167).

The environmentalists lodged their strongest complaint against the absence of time obligations on the OSM when responding to citizen complaints. A West Virginia attorney called this a "glaring defect," noting that, while section 721.13 stipulates that "the office shall conduct an 'inspection' [in response to a citizen complaint], this section fails to provide *when* the inspection shall be conducted!" (C248; emphasis in original). Claiming that the act required "*immediate* inspection," he suggested that "the rule should make this clear" (emphasis in original). A western environmentalist group suggested that the regulation be revised to stipulate that an inspection in response to a citizen complaint "shall occur within ten days from the date of receipt of the information by the [OSM]" (C257). One rationale for such a revision, as suggested earlier, was stated concisely by a representative of the Sierra Club:

> Words such as "within a reasonable time" would leave too much discretion to federal inspectors who will be subjected to the same pressures for lax enforcement as are their state counterparts. [C68]

A comparison of the draft and final interim regulations shows that the more far reaching, fundamental changes made in the latter were consistent with the urgings of environmentalist groups (e.g., the addition of a time limit for inspections triggered by citizen complaints). By contrast, changes made in response to comments and suggestions by the coal industry seem minor and of limited significance and impact. Basically, the word *suspects* was deleted and replaced by *believes* in section 721.13.(a)(1) of the final regulations. The absolute confidentiality of citizen complaints was not preserved, but the only stricture is other federal laws; there is no procedure otherwise for divulging the names of citizen complainants. Finally, whereas the coal industry had favored the requirement that complaints must be written, the final interim regulations recognized the validity of oral complaints, providing they were followed by a written complaint. On balance, the coal industry got relatively little in the revision process; supporters of more stringent regulations were treated more accommodatingly.

Section 842.12 of the proposed permanent regulations is nearly identical to the final interim regulations. The majority of comments OSM received regarding section 842.12 merely repeated those offered in a response to the proposed interim regulations. For example, the AMC-NCA Joint Committee suggested that a citizen complainant should forfeit his right to confidentiality if he accompanied an OSM inspector onto a mine site.

> While it may be that a person who submits a written statement alleging a violation will generally be permitted to keep his identity unknown, once that person exercises his so-called "right of entry" he effectually waives his *regulatory* privilege of confidentiality. An operator is entitled to know who is on his property, and just as it is reasonable and proper for the authorized representative to show appropriate identification, it is equally reasonable the complaining person to do so. OSM's rationale for maintaining confidentiality

must be balanced with the operator's *right* to know who is coming onto his property. [F-507; emphasis in original]

The Joint Committee again raised the question of who would be liable for injuries to a citizen complainant while on a mine site. Once again, the suggested remedy was to require the citizen to sign a written release of the operator "from damages *for any injuries suffered by such person while on mine property*" (F-507; emphasis in original).

When published in 1979, the final permanent regulations essentially were unchanged from the proposed permanent regulations.[11]

## THE AGENCY'S APPROACH TO RULE MAKING

The political process of rule making is, by law, a formal one. Informal negotiations are strictly limited. The system was invented by and for attorneys who wanted to limit inside dealing by the subjects of regulation. Both public hearings and the comment/response process have an adversarial structure. The OSM's enforced compliance style was reflected in the very process of rule making. The agency pushed the formal and adversairal aspects to an extreme. They held the coal industry, the states, and even their own regional managers at arm's length. Only when in serious legal, technical, or political trouble did they modify proposed regulations. Generally they produced tough, detailed, design-based, and legally defensible regulations that would compel direct, enforceable compliance.

The regulations were written by state managers who wished to demonstrate and maintain the agency's independence from capital. They were guided by a spirit of profound distrust for the coal industry. In their view, the law demanded rigid and precise regulations. Neither the political climate nor the economic context stood as a barrier to their actions. They received strong support from the environmentalist community. The time-crunch mandated by the act contributed to the shape of both process and product. A member of the task force told us that

[the OSM's program] was built on the fervor of the times, of the winners. And the winners were the environmental movement people, who had *persisted*. . . . And, by god, they had slain the giant. And the *wicked giant* was lying there. . . . "[Now] the *sinners* are gonna be brought to justice." And they started, "these are gonna be *rigid* regulations, by god. We're not gonna leave anything out. Because you can't trust them. We're gonna write these in great detail."

Similarly, another member of the task force told us, "We wrote those regs as if there had to be fourteen bolts holding down every piece."

# 6 The Inspection and Enforcement Program

Asked to define or to give examples of *law,* most people probably would point to statutes, court decisions, or administrative rulings. They would point to law on the books, which is one way of thinking about law. *Law on the books* threatens, warns, and admonishes us to act or to refrain from acting in certain ways. Law on the books is meant to shape our behavior. But there are always discrepancies of one sort or another between law on the books and law in action, and the way the law is applied to day-to-day life. *Law in action* is another way of thinking about law.

Because law on the books is such an imperfect moulder of behavior, the state creates social control bureaucracies and mandates that they bring law and behavior into closer conformity. For many reasons, the social control apparatus is inadequate for its mandated tasks. Not only do the social control bureaucracies fall short numerically, but also they diverge from their apparent mandate in other ways. It is the worlds and ways of bureaucracy and social control experts that determine law in action. They give purpose and form to law on the books.

It is not enough, then, to examine the construction of law on the books. We must examine how the mandate was implemented in the coal fields and the forces that explain that process. To this point in our analysis, we have focused exclusively on the process of making law on the books. We examined first the process of enacting legislation and, second, the process of promulgating regulations. We now turn our attention to the process of enforcement, to law in action.

## THE GUIDING IDEOLOGY

The protracted and hotly contested congressional battles over strip mining legislation in the 1970s forged narrow, antagonistic beliefs among the combatants. On one side, supporters of legislation were described in the *Mining Congress Journal* as "impassioned crusaders," a small group of "elitists," and a "vociferous and obstinate few" who were accused of "arousing public passions." Their efforts to enact legislation were ridiculed as "simplistic appeals." On the other side, members of environmentalist and citizens' groups likened segments of the coal industry to robber barons, throwbacks to an age of industrial callousness. As they battled the coal industry in Congress, they had employed these assumptions about their adversaries to construct enforcement proposals for the contested legislation.

Anyone in the environmentalists' camp in 1977 who publicly suggested that the coal industry would greet the new federal agency with anything but defiance would have been a laughingstock. Few believed the industry would make a good faith effort to comply. No one seriously believed that appeals to the industry to mend its ways voluntarily would accomplish more than a marginal improvement in reclamation practices. Environmentalists believed that a substantial proportion of mine operators were habitual, hard core offenders of mining regulations. Nothing would be gained by appeals to obey the law cloaked in principles of corporate stewardship or moral obligation. It was widely believed that there was no common ground for negotiating compliance with the law and that mine operators probably would violate these agreements anyway.

These experiences and beliefs caused environmentalists to build their enforcement proposals on deterrence principles. Those who opt for this justification for state controls usually assume that sanction threats, close surveillance, and swift, certain punishment must be the first line of defense against misconduct. This rationale was stated succinctly by an attorney who was instrumental in drafting the SMCRA inspection and enforcement provisions:

> In a regulatory situation where you have a large number of inspectable units [and] . . . significant variations in compliance, including a minority—a significant minority—of inspectable units that simply do not comply, or have a history of noncompliance, . . . You require a mandatory enforcement system. In the Surface Mine Act enforcement system, in almost every one of its provisions—both penalites, cessation orders, NOVs, whatever—is premised on that idea of mandatory enforcement. . . . [I]t may be, in another situation—twenty years down the road, where compliance is up very

high—where you have a growing consensus of behavior [that] . . .
you should drop mandatory enforcement for discretionary enforcement. But . . . we believe mandatory enforcement is justified, and
indeed necessary, in surface mining.

He and his associates favored strict, nondiscretionary enforcement, and
they were successful in crafting statutory enforcement provisions that
reflected their beliefs about the nature of the enforcement task ahead.
The inspection and enforcement sections of Public Law 95–87 are a
strong base on which to build an enforced compliance program.

The act required OSM, during the interim regulatory program, to
conduct unannounced, biannual inspections at every permitted surface
coal mining operation in the United States. As we saw in chapter 5,
private citizens could require an OSM inspection if they suspected that
a mining operation was not in compliance with the regulations (section
517[c]). The act further mandated the issuance of an order to cease all
mining (CO or cessation order) if the violation was not abated in the
allotted time or if the inspector determined that the violation posed a
threat to public health or safety or to the environment (section 521[a][2],
or [3]).

## CREATING AN ENFORCEMENT PROGRAM

Regulatory law is not self-enforcing. Practical application of the rules
entails developing an organization, hiring staff, and constructing enforcement policies. Consequently, one of the OSMRE Task Force's first
objectives was the appointment of an inspection and enforcement (I &
E) task group.

The most influential members of the task group were attorneys, some
of whom had previous experiences battling coal operators. They were
on friendly terms with attorneys in the environmentalists' camp who
drafted much of the I & E language in the act, and there was a free
and easy exchange of ideas among the two groups.

As members of the task group saw it, changing the behavior of mine
operators was no different from influencing the behavior of ordinary
criminal offenders. Principles of deterrence applied to both. They knew
of the industry's history of lawlessness, which they largely attributed to
the states' failure to establish *credible* regulatory programs.

I really came to believe that what was missing [under state regulation]
. . . was just that [coal operators] were not told that "you're supposed

to do it, and this is a serious rule. And it [you don't], we'll just be on your case." . . . I really thought that if we had honest, motivated inspectors, gave them the power and supervised them, and kept our lawyers arguing when they came back, that we would, in fact—you know—people would finally say: "Oh, you mean you're *really* not supposed to put spoil on the downslope? Ah, c'mon. I knew the law said that, but you mean you're really no supposed to do it?" "Yeah," you know. And that was the missing ingredient.

The task group wanted to take the "rule of law" to the coal fields, especially to Appalachia.

Their determination to do so was reinforced by awareness that OSM was to be the primary regulatory authority *only* until the states gained primacy. As a result, members of the I & E task group did not anticipate long-term working relationships with the regulated industry. Instead, they focused on setting precedents for the states to follow. Looking back, a regional manager stated:

> OSM literally had to lead the way, sort of show that this is what was going to be expected in the future when you [the states] get your turn. . . . And you couldn't very well demand that of [the states] if you didn't demand it of yourself.

### The Inspectors

The task group members realized that inspector discretion could ultimately undermine their plans for a policy of enforced compliance. Obviously, the most effective means to guard against enforcement slippage and inconsistencies was to hire inspectors already committed to the enforcement strategies of the headquarters executives. However, when the I & E task group began searching for such personnel, they were forced to move quickly to meet the act's deadline for implementation. Several years later, task force members would look back and see that they were optimistic to believe they could accomplish so much in such a short time. They would wonder if the focus of attention on the worst industry abuses and state shortcomings had shaped a program that was unreasonably stringent. However, such doubts were not reflected in the first-year development of the I & E program.

### Agency Start-up

Drawing on two sources, the I & E task group identified a number of experienced inspectors who shared the agency's enforcement philosophy. OSM headquarters executives identified some candidates through contacts with other federal agencies and former state regulatory managers. Also, names for this pool were sought through informal contacts with a network of attorneys and environmentalists who were active in curbing mining abuses. When OSM's initial budgetary appropriations were delayed, the initial group of inspectors were hired, trained, and supervised by the I & E task group.

The selection of one of OSM's initial inspectors typifies this process. A retired Kentucky state inspector, he had a strong reputation in Appalachia for his knowledge of the industry and his conservationist beliefs. He was hired by OSM after a local attorney introduced him to a leader in the I & E task group. Subsequently, he helped located other former inspectors. The task group followed a similar strategy in the Midwest.

There were strong feelings of camaraderie and commitment among the first group of inspectors. Many of them had experienced frustration in state regulatory programs, and they saw OSM as an opportunity to establish a regulatory program the coal industry would take seriously. Many of them shared the proenvironmental philosophy that produced the act and shaped the interim regulations. Thus, when the OSM began inspecting mine sites in May, 1978, its newly-hired field-level personnel perceived the agency's mission to be protection of the environment by rigorous, nondiscretionary rule enforcement.

Work for the initial OSM inspectors was difficult because agency budget delays created personnel and resource shortages. An "old timer" related this experience to us:

> [W]e would come in on Monday morning and get all of our stuff that we figured we would need from the office, and touch base with the supervisor. Give him a rough itinerary of where we were going to be, and we'd hit the woods. . . . We did all of our certified mailing of citations and all that kind of thing from the [nearest] post office. Did our paperwork at home at night. We were inspecting—a lot of times—from seven in the morning until eight, nine at night.

In addition to the long hours and travel to isolated areas, some inspectors functioned with a limited chain of command or operated out of their own homes.

> [W]e worked more or less out of our houses. It varied from one area to another, depending on how long it took them to find office space and get the phones hooked up, and so on and so forth.

Q: How long did you have to work out of your house?
A: About eight or nine months. . . . All [we] had was field supervisors and inspectors. And we had eleven inspectors, I think, to cover all of [the region].

None of the initial inspectors we interviewed expressed regrets about the decision to adopt an enforced compliance approach. The comments of one inspector provide an interesting metaphor to the OSM's early enforcement period;

In retrospect, I think that . . . the best way to [enforce the regulations] was to put the fear of OSM into the operators right off, at the beginning. And really do a bang-up job, in terms of enforcing the law, so that that would carry over until staffing was complete and . . . housing was found and office space was obtained and equipment issued and so forth. . . . I guess what I'm saying is that it's just like in modern day warfare: one dozen guerilla soldiers can do as much harm or as much good for a campaign as a whole battalion of regular soldiers.

After the regional offices were established, two additional "waves" of new inspectors joined the original group. Some of the later recruits had little coal mining or regulation experience. Many were not as committed as the first wave to an environmental mission. Largely because these recruits were raw, they were especially instructed to avoid negotiation and discretion. As a regional manager put it:

[W]e had some immaturity. We had some people who didn't know a whole hell of a lot about mining. We had to hire a lot of inspectors who . . . didn't have "old heads." They were told: "Goddamn, you're a cop. Get your ass out there and enforce the law."

In the words of a coal operator, OSM's inspectors were "young smart asses who didn't know a dragline from a haul road." Although this belief gained wide acceptance among miners, the facts suggest otherwise. The image of inspectors as greenhorns should not be exaggerated. Data from our mail survey of inspectors indicate that 63 percent had some prior experience in coal mining regulation, and 75 percent had four-year college degrees.[1] Of those with degrees, fully 75 percent were drawn from environmental protection job orientation. However, few inspectors were environmentalists in the ideological sense of the term. Most were country boys—56 percent grew up in rural areas or small towns—from the local region. The majority held conservative political attitudes.[2] Such college-educated state employees are members of a new class that asks that corporations and small business be made accountable. They typically were suspicious of the coal industry and the local state regulatory programs, and they were strongly committed to their work and believed that the federal program was fair and effective.

## INDUSTRY AND STATE OPPOSITION

Even though other provisions of the act had a greater impact on coal producers, the I & E program was the most publicly visible component of the OSM's operations. Inspection and enforcement became a major symbolic issue around which the states and small, economically-marginal operators rallied their resistance efforts. Coal operators depicted inspectors as uninformed about mining, inflexible in their duties, and unreasonable in issuing NOVs for minor infractions. These themes were popular among coal operators in the field and at trade association meetings. For exmple, one regional manager told us:

> [Operators] passed around a story that . . . we had dropped one hundred inspectors on the state . . . and [we] were blitzkreiging the state. And "look for your mine to be inspected," miners were told. "These guys are coming!" I had *five guys* in the whole damn state. . . . See, the truth and what the reputation is are different. And it is the reputation . . . that "these [OSM] guys are like Nazis" [that mine operators reacted to]. Hell, we had cartoons being sent to this office showing an OSM inspector being shot, and it'd say "Pig."

Industry's opposition was strongest in regions that have the highest concentration of small mining operations. These small mine operators were convinced that the OSM was determined to "shut them down." Operators' resistance to the agency assumed a highly visible form in the open defiance of a few individuals in situations like one described by a regional manager:

> [A] small mine operator . . . told me: "I ain't never taken no paper from any Fed. Hell, I've run off EPA, MESA, IRS, and now you guys. I just ain't gonna play your games. This is my land!" Subsequently, he began to be such a symbol of defiance . . . that we sought and received a court order, and with the support of eight to ten armed marshals, we served appropriate notice of his violations

to him on his mine site. The show of force was essential—we used a helicopter and cars—because his men were heavily armed, and he had menaced our inspectors previously.

In some areas, the OSM's inspectos regularly were threatened with physical violence.

At a . . . public hearing at an illegal mine site . . . [the operator] warned that the next time OSM flew over [his] area that [its] helicopter would be shot down. He [reported] that the miners in [his area] are uniting, and there was going to be the same kind of violence that occurred when UMW tried to move into the area. This violence would be directed toward OSM inspectors, because the miners [were] not about to let OSM stop them from feeding their families. A recent helicopter flight, conducted by [state inspection personnel], was hit by small caliber ground fire in this area. [OSM, 1980d]

There were occasional physical assaults on OSM inspectors. Incidents of operator violence usually involved illegal operations—known as "wildcat" mining. Understandably, an operator who has no mining permit is more likely to resist regulatory intervention.

When OSM's inspectors began enforcing the interim program, they tried to conduct their inspections jointly with state personnel. However, with varying speed in the different regions, this practice was discontinued. State opposition to the federal enforcement presence increased even as joint inspections were declining. First, OSM's presence was most strongly resented by those states that were economically dependent on coal. Second, some states believed that OSM's aggressive enforcement policy amounted to criticism of their own performance. Finally, some states objected to any *federal* presence: a belief that states have the legal right to handle such matters without interference from Washington. The states' attacks on the federal I & E program found a receptive audience in the coal industry. Industry attacks on the federal I & E program were reinforced by state resistance efforts. Eventually the two groups sounded similar complaints about "overzealous" federal inspectors.

## EVALUATION OF ENFORCEMENT

Basic data on the OSM's varying levels of enforcement activities are shown in Table 6-1. The rise of citations (both NOVs and COs) during the early years was followed by a sharp drop under the Reagan administration. The volume of citations during the Carter administration far exceeded the number issued by the various state programs.

The coal industry complained, but it was the environmentalists who most carefully examined the agency's performance of inspections. They criticized the OSM for failure to conduct semiannual inspections of every U.S. mine site during the interim program. During the first seven months of operations (May-December 1978), the agency inspected only 10 percent of the nation's inspectable units. In the subsequent six-month period (January-July 1979), the OSM's inspection rate increased to 25 percent. Between June of 1979 and March of 1980, the agency had conducted complete inspections for only 50 percent of the 15,591 permitted mine sites (U.S. Congress, House, 1980:431).[3]

An investigation of enforcement at a sample of forty-eight mines located in five western states revealed a similar pattern of shortcomings in the issuance of notices of violation.[4] The Surface Mining Act requires that citations must be written whenever a violation is observed and that it be issued immediately. OSM inspectors reported a total of 464 violative conditions during their inspections at the sample mines; however, notices of violation were issued for only 48.7 percent of the total (226 NOVs). Of the 226 NOVs issued, only 82.7 percent were issued on the mine site (Johnson et al., 1980).

Our analysis of the OSM application of penalties demonstrates a similar pattern of discrepancy between statutory mandate and the agency's performance.[5] We selected a purposive sample of eighty-three coal mining companies in two of OSM's five regions (Appalachia and the West). Each mining company received at least one NOV during the period from October, 1978 through March, 1980. The sample was drawn to ensure approximately equal numbers of NOVs for small, medium, and large firms. The eighty-three firms received a total of 735 NOVs during the eighteen months. We found that relatively small fines were imposed for the majority of NOVs.[6] The average fine was $1,027, and the maximum fine imposed was $4,500. No fine was imposed in 264 cases (39.1 percent). We also determined that only 301 NOVs completed the penalty process.[7]

## SANCTIONING CORPORATE OFFENDERS

As a final step in our analysis, we examined the relationship between company size and fines assessed by the OSM. Drawing from the research literature on the sanctioning of ordinary offenders,[8] we employed two categories of independent variables that conceivably affect the magnitude of the civil penalty: legal and extra-legal. *Legal* variables are those

**TABLE 6-1**
OSM INSPECTION SUMMARY—JULY 1978 TO JUNE 1982

| Time Period | Number of Inspections | Notices of Violation | Cessation Orders | Citizen Complaints |
|---|---|---|---|---|
| Jul 78 - Dec 78 | 2,585 | 539 | 116 | 10 |
| Jan 79 - Jun 79 | 5,901 | 1,469 | 274 | 225 |
| Jul 79 - Dec 79 | 14,405 | 2,993 | 541 | 497 |
| Jan 80 - Jun 80 | 19,569 | 3,797 | 812 | 546 |
| Jul 80 - Dec 80 | 19,107 | 3,165 | 821 | 530 |
| Jan 81 - Jun 81 | 13,519 | 1,330 | 396 | 424 |
| Jul 81 - Dec 81 | 13,551 | 1,038 | 222 | 402 |
| Jan 82 - Jun 82 | 8,825 | 693 | 192 | 259 |

*Source:* Office of Surface Mining

"factors emphasized in official-normative descriptions of the criminal justice system, such as the seriousness of a defendant's offense, the nature of his previous criminal record, and the degree of 'viciousness' manifested in the offense" (Hagan, 1974:358). *Extra-legal* variables are those presumed to be legally irrelevant to the imposition of sentence, such as the defendant's race, sex, age, and socioeconomic status. We employed three legal variables in the analysis. For each violation, we determined the *assessed negligence* of the corporate offender,[9] *assessed damage* of the activity,[10] and *seriousness* of the violation.[11] The data permitted the use of only one extra-legal independent variable: the *size* of the mining corporation.[12]

We were interested primarily in determining the nature and relative magnitude that our legal and extra-legal variables made to the size of corporate fines. We used path analytic procedures to examine the direction and strength of the relationships between variables in our model.

Our research examines a "tightly coupled system"; that is, a system in which law, regulations, detection of violations, and sanctions are closely conjoined.[13] Two of our legal measures—assessed damage and assessed negligence—are among four used by OSM's assessors to determine corporate fines. Thus, the determinative impact of these legal variables necessarily will be quite strong. Under these conditions, any contribution to explained variance must be viewed as substantively significant.

Figure 6-1 shows the results of the path analysis. As expected for the reasons previously indicated, the coefficient of determination is quite large (.70). The legal variables are strong, equal predictors of the size of the fine (Beta = .48 for assessed damage; .55 for assessed negligence). Our measure of seriousness has no determinative impact when the remaining variables are controlled. This finding suggests that our extra-legal variable, company size, is a significant determinant of the size of the fine even after the closely coupled legal variables have been controlled (Beta = .10). Although company size contributes only one percent to the explained variance, it remains statistically significant and theoretically interesting as well. Despite a rigorous effort by the OSM to eliminate bias from the sanctioning process, large companies enjoy a modest advantage in the sanctioning process. In addition, large companies benefit slightly in the assessment of penalties by virtue of the more limited damage wrought by their violations.

During the time period reported in our analysis, the OSM enforced regulations closely tied to its enabling legislation. Inspectors were bound by promulgated regulations, and OSM's penalty system was sharply constrained by law, regulations, and inspection procedures. The size of

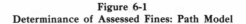

Figure 6-1
Determinance of Assessed Fines: Path Model

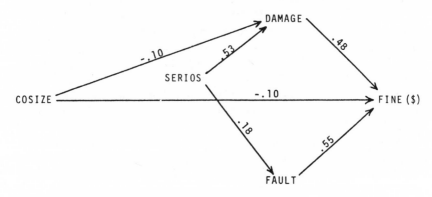

Where: FINE is the Magnitude of the Assessed Fine (in $)
DAMAGE is the Degree of Assessed Damage
FAULT is the Degree of Assessed Negligence
SERIOS is the Seriousness of the Violative Conduct
COSIZE is the Size of the Offending Corporation (trichotomized)

the assessed fine reflects a concerted effort to rationalize the penalty system so that it is directly tied to legal and regulatory mandates. This tight coupling is a result of the technocratic, legalistic constraints operating during the period of agency formation. Even though OSM's regional offices were relatively autonomous in their daily operations (loosely coupled to headquarters), the central Assessment Office represents an attempt to guard against discretionary variances in the application of the law.

The fact that company size influences the amount of the fine, even though minimally, suggests the presence of informal mechanisms of corporate influence on agency decision making. A most likely source of bias is the field inspector. On the basis of a variety of data, it appears that larger mining companies benefit from the fact that inspector-client confrontations are a match between salaried technicians, where large, not small, industry has the upper hand.

In Table 6-2 we show the relationship between company size and payment of fines. As can be seen, there is a strong relationship between the two variables; larger companies are substantially more likely than smaller companies to pay their fines. Because larger companies tend to be more conscious of adverse publicity and the avoidance of a tarnished corporate reputation, they are more likely to pay their fines than smaller competitors, whose images are not presented to a large public and corporate audience.

Examination of the OSM's efforts to collect civil fines also suggests that the penalty process did not function as its planners anticipated.[14] By October of 1981, the OSM either had proposed or finalized assessments for $34,514,968.48. Of this sum, only $3,498,144.87 had been collected (about 10 percent). Department of Justice data indicate that as of May, 1982, a total of 1,373 cases had been referred by the OSM for collection of civil penalties. Of this total, 52.3 percent (718 cases) still had not been filed with the federal courts. Partial or complete payment had been made in only 10.5 percent (144) of the 1,373 cases. The courts had issued judgments in an additional 15.4 percent of the cases, but they remained in various stages of the collection process (U.S. Department of Justice, letter, 6 May 1982).

Clearly, the agency did not plan for the sheer magnitude of the penalty collection task. These problems were exacerbated by the difficulty of locating many of the cited individuals and corporations, especially in Appalachia. These individuals often incorporate under one name, operate for a short period of time, and then dissolve their business. Later, when the coal market "picks up," they incorporate again under a new name. Obviously, the task of locating and securing payment from such operators is difficult. Inevitably, the rather poor record of collection calls into question the deterrent effectiveness of the threatened civil penalties. There is more than a touch of irony in the fact that OSM's penalty process encountered the same kinds of problems previously experienced by other regulatory agencies.[15]

## IMPLICATIONS

Extreme distrust of the coal industry and past experience with lax state regulation led the proponents of federal control of surface mining

**TABLE 6–2**
**RELATIONSHIP BETWEEN COMPANY SIZE AND WHETHER ASSESSED FINE WAS PAID**

| Evidence Fine Was Paid? | Company Size | | | Total |
|---|---|---|---|---|
| | Small | Medium | Large | |
| Yes | 38.3% | 67.7% | 81.8% | 60.1% |
| | (46) | (63) | (72) | (181) |
| No | 61.7 | 32.3 | 18.2 | 39.9 |
| | (74) | (30) | (16) | (120) |

Gamma = -.59

to incorporate specific enforcement mandates in the legislation. The managers of inspection and enforcement in the OSM brought to their task a strong commitment to insuring obeisance to law in the coal fields. They viewed local state regulators as having been too deferential to local coal operators in enforcing state laws. Wishing to avoid the possibility of bending the law at the point of application, they developed a program that would limit inspector discretion and negotiation at the mine site. The program was intended to be rule-based and stringent. Efforts were made to hire personnel who would be committed to this program. In practice, full implementation of inspection and enforcement was limited by available resources. In general the inspectors followed the intent of the program, although their actions showed a slight bias favoring large firms. The inspection and enforcement program's enforced compliance style was intended to prevent any watering down of the law or capture of the agency at the grass roots. A rigorous implementation program was the final stage in establishing the relative autonomy of the regulatory agency.

# 7 Regional Variation in Inspection and Enforcement

Because of the wide variation among state surface mining codes and enforcement capability, the Office of Surface Mining was strongly committed to a strategy of enforced compliance. State differences in enforcement were produced by the diversity across regions in mining conditions and in the strength of the coal industry. In the face of these constraints, the Washington office of the OSM was *not* able to apply the law or to execute grass roots enforcement uniformly across all regions. In this chapter, we explain why distinctive enforcement styles emerged in two quite diverse regions. The organization of regional styles was influenced by variables external to policy mandates and by the daily routines of field-level inspectors.

## REGULATORY ENFORCEMENT STYLES

Regulatory enforcement is a means of controlling or "policing" behavior. Consequently, there are natural parallels between regulators and police. All controllers are faced with the problems of applying legal rules to specific cases. Since rules often have ambiguous boundaries and referents and are subject to conflicting interpretations, strict or literal enforcement is nearly impossible. Moreover, enforcement resources nearly always are insufficient to handle the volume and complexity of violations. In practice, law is socially constructed, and the variant forms of control are shaped by contextual factors.

Research on the police has given us an embryonic understanding of the ways departments vary across communities and of the social contexts that elicit different types of organizational responses (Reiss and Bordua, 1967; Gardiner, 1969; Manning, 1977, 1980; Wilson, 1978). There is a lesson here for students of regulatory law enforcement: regulatory bureaucracies and operations are tied to the social matrix in which they operate. Like police officers, regulatory personnel are not entirely free to develop idiosyncratic styles of enforcement behavior. Rather, the "selection" of a dominant organizational enforcement style is influenced by the larger contextual arrangements in which the inspectors operate (Nivola, 1978; Thomas, 1980). Observers of the regulatory process have distinguished different types of regulatory law enforcement (Thomas, 1980; Kagan, 1980; Bardach and Kagan, 1982; Kagan and Scholz, 1984; Hawkins, 1984). Running through many of the analyses of regulatory enforcement is a distinction between two styles.

An enforced compliance style is characteristic of inspectors who approach their work very much like police officers. Their orientation and approach is punitive. This rule-oriented approach reflects the belief that strict, uniform enforcement will deter violators and maximize compliance. Rule-oriented inspectors issue citations for every violation they observe during inspections. Correspondingly, they minimize the use of negotiational enforcement strategies, such as consultation and bargaining. In sum, this style of enforcement is rule-based.

By contrast, other inspectors employ a negotiated compliance style. Emphasizing a results-oriented approach, they are flexible and stress responsiveness, forbearance, and the transmission of information. Primary reliance on the strict, uniform application of formal sanctions is considered less effective than negotiation as a method to secure compliance. Conciliatory inspectors may employ trade-offs, gaming tactics, and cajoling to gain compliance from violators and potential violators.

At the field-level of enforcement of the Surface Mining Act, regulatory styles varied *between* regions and *within* regions. Our analysis focuses on the emergence of enforced compliance in one region (which we label *Region East*) and of negotiated compliance in another region (which we label *Region West*).

## BACKGROUND

In Region East, located in the heart of Appalachia, coal is mined on relatively steep mountain slopes, in narrow valleys, and under heavy annual rainfall. By contrast, Region West has level or rolling terrain and rainfall is scarce. In general, environmentally sound mining practices are more difficult and more costly in Region East.

Other important regional differences are evident in the pattern of ownership and production. In Region East, nearly all mining rights are privately owned, and much of the surface mining is done by numerous small firms. The majority of western coal deposits are owned by the federal government, the railroads, or Native American tribes. Because so much coal in Region West is controlled by the federal government, western mining companies were accustomed to a federal presence even prior to enactment of Public Law 95-87. These large corporations operate enormous surface mines that provide low-sulfur coal to electric utilities under long-term contracts. As a rule, western mines employ regulatory "professionals" who function as in-house inspectors tracking the operation's compliance with regulatory programs.

Finally, there were large differences between regions in the strength of the typical state program. Hostility toward state regulatory programs and personnel was quite common among some Appalachian coal operators. Wildcat mining has been a problem in some areas of Appalachia. Environmental abuses and ineffective state regulation there provided much of the impetus for passage of federal surface mining legislation. In the West, state regulatory authorities and programs have enjoyed a reputation for honesty and stringency superior to their Appalachian counterparts and wildcat mining is virtually unknown.

## CONTRASTS IN REGIONAL ENFORCEMENT ACTIVITY

Despite the formal, hierarchical relationship between Washington and the regional offices and the strict enforced compliance ideology of the main office, the regional directors retained considerable autonomy. OSM personnel in regions East and West developed different enforcement styles. The approach in Region East emphasized enforced compliance, while Region West developed a negotiated compliance approach. These differences are evidenced in official statistics on OSM's enforcement activities and also in our interview and questionnaire data.

### Statistical Data[1]

During 1979-1980, Region East employed sixty certified, field-level inspectors, while Region West employed only seven. In 1981, there were 6,689 "inspectable units" in Region East, but only 161 comparable units in Region West (OSM, 1981).[2] Given the substantial difference in these numbers, it would be expected that Region East inspectors would issue many more NOVs and COs than inspectors in Region West. In fact this is what happened. During the specified time period, Region East issued 3,254 NOVs and 901 COs, while Region West issued 88 and 5 respectively. When we convert the number of NOVs and COs to rates of enforcement, we find that Region East issued 54.23 NOVs and 15.02 COs per inspector, while Region West issued only 12.14 NOVs and 0.71 COs per inspector.

Alternatively, we calculated rates of enforcement activity by employing the total number of completed inspections. During 1981, Region East inspectors completed 12,451 inspections, while Region West inspectors completed 378 inspections. The resulting rates of enforcement were 2.62 NOVs and 0.73 COs per ten inspections in Region East and 2.34 NOVs and 0.14 COs in Region West.

A final comparative measure employs as a base the amount of coal produced in each region.[3] For the period of mid-1979 to mid-1980, coal operators in Region East produced 189.01 million tons of coal, while operators in Region West produced 200.96 million tons of coal (U.S. Dept. of Energy, 1981; 1981a). Using these production figures as a base, inspectors in Region East issued 17.22 NOVs and 4.77 COs per million tons of coal produced. At the same time, inspectors in Region West issued only 0.44 NOVs and 0.03 COs per million tons of coal produced. Table 7-1 provides a summary of the various measures, including comparable statistics, for all OSM regions.

## Interview and Questionnaire Data[4]

In view of their different histories and production problems, we may assume that one reason for regional variation in inspection and enforcement activity is real differences in the incidence and prevalence of illegal mining practices. Unfortunately, this interpretation only shifts the problem of understanding. We *still need* to determine how regulatory personnel interpret objective differences in mining practices and violations and how they convert these interpretations into distinctive enforcement styles.

As the foregoing statistical data suggest, a program of vigorous, rule-oriented enforcement took shape in Region East. An inspector there told us that OSM "started out . . . like a bunch of SS troops." Region East inspectors were imbued with a philosophy of firm, impartial enforcement and were encouraged to apply the regulations in a quite literal fashion, as another inspector explained:

> When you put the hard hat on and get out of the truck on that mine site, you've got to be like a state cop out there. You've got

**TABLE 7-1**

**SUMMARY MEASURES OF OSM INSPECTION AND ENFORCEMENT ACTIVITY, JULY 1, 1979, TO JUNE 30, 1980**

| Region | Number of NOVs Per: | | | Number of COs Per: | | |
| | Inspector | Ten Inspections | Million Short Tons of Coal[a] | Inspector | Ten Inspections | Million Short Tons of Coal[a] |
|---|---|---|---|---|---|---|
| East | 54.23 | 2.62 | 17.22 | 15.02 | 0.73 | 4.77 |
| West | 12.14 | 2.34 | 0.44 | 0.71 | 0.14 | 0.03 |
| Total (U.S.) | 42.70 | 2.01 | 8.45 | 8.51 | 0.40 | 1.66 |

[a] U.S. Department of Energy, 1981, 1981a.

> to enforce the law. No more, or no less. . . . At least that's the
> way this office is run. That's the way they're all run in this district
> and in this region.

Because relatively little emphasis was placed on the need for and the desirability of discretion and flexibility, enforcement in Region East manifested important features of the enforced compliance style discussed earlier.

Whereas a rule-orientation was characteristic of Region East, Region West managers opted for the results-orientation of negotiated compliance. From the outset, western managers viewed the SMCRA and the regulations as flexible resources. Vigorous, uniform rule enforcement was played down as a necessary or desirable strategy. In Region West, relatively greater emphasis was placed on conciliatory enforcement and efforts to work accommodatingly with mine operators. One inspector commented on the enforcement style of the western regional director:

> I heard him speak one time in a citizens' group meeting and say:
> "Look, I understand in the East why they [OSM] 'hit the ground
> running,' but I don't deal with jackleg coal miners. . . . I deal with
> these multi-million dollar operations. So I'm going to be very cau-
> tious."

We reasoned that regional differences in inspector's legalistic and conciliatory orientations would be reflected in regional variation in questionnaire responses. In the questionnaire we included two scales designed to measure these differences: a *legalistic scale* and a *conciliatory scale*. Table 7–2 summarizes the results of the questionnaire measures.[5] Consistent with expectations, Region East personnel scored substantially higher on the legalistic scale than did their counterparts in Region West (mean scores of 4.95 and 2.33, respectively). Contrary to our expectations, however, there was no appreciable difference between the two regions in inspectors' scores on the conciliatory scale (9.18 in Region East and 9.33 in Region West).

Although we are puzzled by the regions' comparable scores on the conciliatory scale, several possible explanations for this come to mind.[6] First, because OSM was a new agency, it may have been extremely difficult for Region East inspectors to avoid completely the use of some consultation and education in their enforcement routines. There is, in fact, a good deal of interview data to suggest the validity of this interpretation. For example, a Region East inspector told us:

**TABLE 7-2**

**REGIONAL VARIATION ON DIMENSIONS OF REGULATORY ENFORCEMENT STYLES**

| Dimension | Region East | | | Region West | | | U. S. Total | | |
|---|---|---|---|---|---|---|---|---|---|
| | X̄ Score | S.D. | N | X̄ Score | S.D. | N | X̄ Score | S.D. | N |
| Legalistic[a] | 4.95 | 3.05 | 44 | 2.33 | 1.63 | 6 | 4.59 | 2.57 | 126 |
| Conciliatory[b] | 9.18 | 1.82 | 44 | 9.33 | 2.07 | 6 | 8.51 | 2.35 | 126 |

[a] A three-item scale (Cronbach's alpha = .67). Items are as follows: "Generally the requirement that OSM inspectors write a NOV on every violation they observe is not an effective regulatory strategy" [0 Strongly Agree; 1 Agree; 2 Undecided; 3 Disagree; 4 Strongly Disagree]; "The best way for inspectors to do their job is to go strictly 'by the book'" [4 Strongly Agree; 3 Agree; 2 Undecided; 1 Disagree; 0 Strongly Disagree]; and "I have tried to enforce the interim regulations strictly and uniformly, much as a police officer would do" [4 Strongly Agree; 3 Agree; 2 Undecided; 1 Disagree; 0 Strongly Disagree]. Responses to the three items were summed.

[b] A three-item scale (Cronbach's alpha = .77). Items are as follows: "Compliance with the regulations is easiest to obtain if the inspector advises and works to educate the operator"; "In my work I have tried primarily to educate and consult with coal operators"; and "The best way for inspectors to do their job is to consult with and try to educate mine operators." Response alternatives to all three items were as follows: [4 Strongly Agree; 3 Agree; 2 Undecided; 1 Disagree; and 0 Strongly Disagree]. Responses to the three items were summed.

I've had some [mine sites] where I go out there and make the inspection and find he's not even started on it yet, still buttoning up his last job. And he's not started on the area I intended to inspect. And that's a sterling opportunity to take him by the hand and go out there to the area that he's going to mine and say: "now, you're permitted [mine permit] for a silt pond down here, . . . and this is the way I want it constructed, just like the plans say. Now if you're going to have a problem with this, . . . need a board baffle in there and you want to change that to rock, it's easier to do. But these are things you need to be thinking about before you start in there and get yourself all sideways." . . . "You're doing the work I've told you on your other jobs but . . . get the permit changed so you can stay straight before you get wrong. Do it right the first time."

Second, because they deal with a more heterogenous group of operators than does Region West, eastern inspectors may have had a specific type of operator in mind when they responded to the questionnaire items. On one hand, they may have endorsed the highly legalistic approach to enforcement because they were fully aware of a group of willful violators—"amoral calculators" (Kagan and Scholz, 1984). On the other hand, eastern inspectors may have scored high on the conciliatory scale because they were also cognizant of operators whose noncompliance resulted from ignorance or ineptitude—"organizational incompetents" (Kagan and Scholz, 1984).

## ANALYSIS

Our interpretation of the regional variation in enforcement styles highlights the importance of regional differences in three areas: (1) regulatory tasks (2) employee experiences with and beliefs about coal operators and state regulatory programs, and (3) political environments.

### Regulatory Tasks

Inspection and enforcement personnel in regions East and West were mandated by the act to perform identical tasks: inspection of surface coal mines. Regional managers and personnel were aware of headquarters' preference for a legalistic enforcement style and of the efforts by headquarters executives to determine if they were pursuing violations vigorously. However, the equality of the regulatory task obscures very real differences in the social organization of mining and inspecting in regions

East and West. These differences are of such a nature that they created divergence in the nature and difficulty of the tasks inspectors in the two regions were expected to perform.

One variation in the performance of regulatory tasks resulted from the manner in which regions East and West handled the permit process. Even during the interim program, the states retained responsibility for issuing mining permits. Because of the presence of federal coal, Region West presented the only deviation from this arrangement. To a great extent, Region West personnel used their control over the mine permit process as an enforcement tool. They were able to employ permit reviews to extract promises of sound reclamation practices from potential mine operators. Because they lacked control over permitting, other regions relied more extensively on conventional inspection and enforcement procedures.

In addition, the two regions are characterized by dissimilar mine-staffing patterns. Because the mines in Region West are large, their organization and staffing patterns are more complex than in Region East.

> Most of the mines in the West have a resident environmental specialist, either at the mine or at least someone who is assigned those duties. A lot of the larger mines—most of them, in fact— have people who are trained in regulatory compliance function. And those are the people you deal with. The people back in the East . . . that you deal with are the pit foreman or the mine superintendent. . . . You're dealing more with production-oriented people in the East. And in the West, most of the people you deal with are not *production* oriented, but environmentally oriented.

These specialized reclamation personnel often monitor developments in the regulatory matrix in which mining is conducted, stay abreast of advances and alternatives in reclamation practices, and plan for reclamation in a legal, cost-effective manner. These specialized personnel are salaried, technical peers of OSM inspectors, are generally well-educated, and tend to accept the principle, if not the substance, of regulation. Also, they possess a long-range understanding of mining and reclamation plans on particular mine sites. They can demonstrate to the inspector how apparent deviations from the regulations are integral parts of comprehensive plans or are alternative methods for accomplishing reclamation objectives. In a word, specialized personnel are much more likely to be civil and reasonable toward inspectors.

The picture is very different in Region East. When inspectors arrive at an eastern mine site, they are more likely to encounter production personnel than specialists. Production workers tend to be poorly educated, to lack a detailed understanding of the regulations, and to be unsympathetic toward any interference with production activities and schedules.

> Q: What are the relative advantages and disadvantages, from the inspector's standpoint, of having to deal with production people, as opposed to specialists in reclamation?
>
> A: [T]he production people—you have to explain, reexplain. He doesn't even know what part of the regulations you're talking about. The reclamation guy, that's his job. I mean, you don't even have to—probably—cite the regulations. He knows it. In other words, he *knows* he may be incorrect. Or he knows how to articulate, "Gee, I'm trying to do this instead of doing that, so I'm not in violation." He knows how to properly . . . articulate the argument against some sort of enforcement action. . . . Or, he can demonstrate, "here's what we're doing, here's how the mine will proceed." . . . He can sort of look into the future, and look at what you've done since the last time [the inspector] was there. He can demonstrate what they did. He's *knowledgable* of those regs. Production guy—I mean, I've been on sites with inspectors where some of the *simplest* violations . . . had to be explained ten times. Often [the] production guy will take his reclamation plan and never look at it. Throw it in the truck, that's it.
>
> Q: Its much easier to deal with specialists?
>
> A: Right.
>
> Q: Makes the job more manageable and, I would imagine, just less of a headache?
>
> A: Oh yeah, Oh yeah. Oh yeah, that's for sure. Even if you get in an argument, I think it's less of a headache. At least you're arguing with someone who can articulate with you and speak to you on the level of the regulations.

Specialized personnel pose a special kind of threat to OSM inspectors, as an inspector told us:

> [Back in the East], with small operators, it [is] more of a "down home attitude." . . . Good-ole-boy approach. Whereas out here, when you're dealing with . . . a person in every specific field, you're much more on your guard for technical issues . . . than just . . . a broad, sweep-of-the-hand type approach.
>
> Q: Do the large companies ever intimidate you just because they have so many experts in every different field?
>
> A: Sure.
>
> Q: How do you deal with that?
>
> A: Well, I personally am more careful. When I'm writing a violation, I'm real careful that I have "the goods," so to speak, before I

act. But the problem out here is a lot of the people that you're dealing with have a better technical understanding of the problems than perhaps I do.

Q: Well, what do you do in that case, just concede to a greater amount of knowledge?

A: Well, I think in some cases I probably do realistically. . . . It's pretty hard to try to . . . argue about a specific situation and you don't know as much about it as the person you're arguing with.

On both counts then—because specialized personnel are reasonable *and* knowledgable—Region West inspectors may approach their duties with a degree of deference, circumspection and, therefore, conciliation, which is less common in Region East.

The lessons here, while comonplace, are important nonetheless. First, a civil clientele begets a civil, conciliatory enforcement style. Conversely, an angry, disrespectful, or defiant clientele begets a more aggressive, determined enforcement style, on the assumption that only by such actions can future problems of a similar nature be deterred (Reiss, 1971). Second, regulatory encounters in which the enforcement agent feels less knowledgeable than the other party contain the potential for overly deferential and, therefore, lenient treatment.

## Employee Experiences and Beliefs

Diversity in the nature of regulatory tasks does not fully explain all the variation in the two regional enforcement styles. Employee experiences with and beliefs about coal operators and state regulatory programs also play a part.

Managerial personnel in the two regions took their positions fully aware of the regional differences in surface mining. Those placed in Region East were fully cognizant of the historical record of weak enforcement and operators' recalcitrance in Appalachia. Many Region East supervisors and managers had prior experience with the Apalachian coal industry; a portion of them had experienced the frustrations of working for state regulatory programs in Appalachia. A number of them viewed OSM employment as an opportunity to set new state regulation precedents.

They operated under no illusions about the ease of their task. A certain resistance to any form of external interference was seen as almost second nature in some areas of Appalachia.

> In the mountains, they are an independent, very independent people. They don't appreciate anyone . . . coming up there and saying, "Now you've got to do this." They look at it that you're encroaching on something that's none of your business. Their attitude is "this is my land. I'll do with it what I darn well please." And they'll go so far as to say, "As long as it's not hurting anyone else, then why are you up here hassling me about it?"

In addition to an awareness of this general antipathy toward external interference, supervisors and inspectors alike were aware of the existence of a group of operators considered to be "hard-core nonconformists." Some of these operators had threatened or assaulted state inspectors in the past with relative impunity.

> [Y]ou've got [one kind of operator] that practically won't talk to you at all. . . . You really feel uncomfortable around them 'cause . . . you're afraid they're going over the edge any minute. They practically won't talk to you and consider you to be a Communist and everthing else. . . . Your wildcat category is where these kind of operators fall.

While incidents of physical assaults on Region East's inspectors were not common, they were significantly higher than in the West. Confrontations like the following incident prompted eastern OSM managers to call in law enforcement officials to protect inspectors during visits to remote mining sites.

> On March 7, Robert Hatmaker assaulted Bill McCreary, an OSM inspector. . . . Hatmaker apparently threatened McCreary, who did not budge [from his car]. Hatmaker then opened McCreary's car door, and when he couldn't pull him out because the seat belt was fastened, he repeatedly punched McCreary in the face. [*Mountain Life and Work*, June 1980:37]

Between 1978 and 1982, U.S. attorneys initiated criminal prosecution in twelve cases of such physical assault on Region East inspectors. No similar cases were referred to the Department of Justice by Region West. OSM's Region East personnel saw their task, in part, as one of curbing this segment of the industry by bringing the rule of law to the Appalachian coal fields. Region East managers believed that aggressive, consistent enforcement against known violators would enhance the operators' perceptions of the credibility and legitimacy of OSM and its operations. One Region East manager explained:

> [O]ur philosophy was "worst case operators" first—ones the states wouldn't go on. . . . It's sort of like beating up the bully on the block. Take on the bully on the block. Beat him up real good . . . and then half your problems are over because word gets out.

Because of the existence of informal communication networks, such enforcement activities would eventually convince operators that the OSM, unlike state authorities, would not simply "go away."

In addition to their general suspicion of state regulators and segments of the coal industry, Region East personnel realized that many operators possessed limited education and rarely planned their mining beyond a few days or weeks. OSM personnel faced the major task of informing and educating such operators. In short, OSM personnel began their work with the assumptions that state regulation had been ineffective or corrupt, that many operators would resist their actions, and that the job would be difficult. Only an aggressive enforcement program would cause coal operators to take OSM's program seriously.

Although differences should not be overstated, personnel in Region West began their work with a different set of assumptions. They understood that western coal producers were accustomed to stringent regulation, and perceived regulation itself as a legitimate governmental function. Consequently, Region West personnel did not anticipate a high level of operator resistance to their efforts. In the West, mining managers are usually college educated, and long-range planning is an integral part of the mining process. Furthermore, there is no evidence to suggest the existence of any significant level of operator defiance in the West, as there has been in Appalachia.

Region west personnel also assumed a higher overall level of good faith on the part of coal operators who, it was believed, were interested in mining in an environmentally sound way and in avoiding adverse publicity.

> Most of the mines out here are rather large mines. There are very few small ones. . . . For instance, we're talking about mines with several thousands of acres involved, as compared to mines back East that have less than one acre. Now the people that run these mines are large companies mostly, and public opinion is very important to these outfits. . . . The working relationships we had with the operators here were much different than those relationships back in

Appalachia. . . . So you don't have the failure to abate situations that arise in the East.

Evidence suggests that in some important respects personnel in regions East and West retained quite different beliefs about the coal industry and the adequacy of state-level regulation. In our mail questionnaire, we asked several questions to assess inspectors' perceptions of the trustworthiness of coal operators and state regulatory authorities. Table 7.3 summarizes responses to three questions about these issues and areas. As can be seen, the results were consistent on all three measures. Region East inspectors generally were more suspicious of coal operators, perceived a higher level of willful noncompliance, and were more fearful of an erosion of industry compliance after the states acquired regulatory primacy.

## Political Environment

Diversity in the performance of regulatory tasks and disparate employee attitudes toward the coal industry and state programs were influential factors in shaping regional enforcement styles. However, the principal determinants of enforcement style variations between the two regions were a number of differences in local political conditions. Generally industry's criticism of OSM was considerably more intense in Region East than in Region West. Many Appalachian operators viewed western mines as an economic threat and embraced a conspiratorial view of OSM and its relationship with the large mining companies.[7] In the eyes of Appalachian operators, OSM was working in concert with western producers to eliminate eastern competition. As one Region East operator suggested:

> They [western coal producers] can't market their coal against our coal. So they use the federal government to put the clamps on us in order for them to build the market up for their coal.

Such beliefs are widespread among smaller Appalchian coal producers (Lynxwiler and Groce, 1981).

Historically, the coal industry has been a major source of government revenue in Appalachia. Coal operators were aware of their importance to state economies and frequently used the threat of relocation to maintain rationale for enactment of SMCRA. After OSM began operations, the

## TABLE 7-3
### REGIONAL DIFFERENCES AMONG INSPECTORS IN PERCEPTIONS OF COAL OPERATORS AND STATE REGULATORY AUTHORITIES

| Perceptions of: | Region East | | | Region West | | | U. S. Total | | |
|---|---|---|---|---|---|---|---|---|---|
| | $\bar{X}$ Score | S.D. | N | $\bar{X}$ Score | S.D. | N | $\bar{X}$ Score | S.D. | N |
| Degree of Willful Noncompliance by Coal Operators[a] | 1.70 | 0.63 | 44 | 0.83 | 0.41 | 6 | 1.59 | 0.70 | 126 |
| Coal Operators' Trustworthiness[b] | 1.05 | 0.91 | 44 | 1.33 | 0.82 | 6 | 1.20 | 0.98 | 126 |
| Distrust of State Regulatory Authorities[c] | 2.61 | 0.97 | 44 | 1.83 | 0.75 | 6 | 2.59 | 0.98 | 126 |

[a] "Based on your personal experience, how often do mine operators willfully and knowingly violate the federal regulations?" [3 Very Frequently; 2 Frequently; 1 Infrequently; 0 Almost Never]

[b] "Most coal operators can be trusted to do the right thing and to mine their coal in an environmentally sound way." [3 Strongly Agree; 3 Agree; 2 Undecided; 1 Disagree; 0 Strongly Disagree]

[c] "Most of the progress that OSM has made toward curbing mining abuses will be lost when state regulatory programs are implemented." [4 Strongly Agree; 3 Agree; 2 Undecided; 1 Disagree; 0 Strongly Disagree]

various states in Region East attacked it, fearing the harm it could cause to regional coal operators, employment, and tax revenues. The picture is different in Region West. While the western states have attacked the federal regulatory presence, it has been in the context of the more generalized "Sagebrush Rebellion." This movement by westerners and their state representatives casts the federal government in the role of a greedy, insensitive owner of large tracts of western land that usurps the states' right to use and develop the land for their own purposes. In this context, attacks on OSM lost much of their special focus.

Finally, in Region East, OSM began operations against an historical backdrop of considerable indigenous citizen opposition to the excesses of surface coal mining. Because much of the strip mining in Appalachia is conducted adjacent to homes or rural settlements, the environmental, social, and property damage from this type of mining has harmed many citizens. Moreover, in Appalachia grass roots movements openly express concern over the perceived venality and powerlessness of state regulatory authorities. When OSM arrived on the scene, citizens were urged to exercise their rights under SMCRA and told that only by doing so would past abuses be corrected and curbed (Center for Law and Social Policy, 1978). For example, one Appalachian group filed a 1979 suit to force OSM to comply with the act by developing an aggressive, literal enforcement program (Council of the Southern Mountains, Inc. et al. v. Andrus, U.S. Dist. Court, D.C., Civil Action #79-1521).

There is a clear, substantial difference between regions East and West in the number of citizen complaints about harmful or dangerous mining practices. During 1979-1980, Region East received 445 citizen complaints, while Region West received only five. In Table 7-4, we converted the number of citizen complaints to a rate that makes comparison across regions more meaningful. The data in Table 7-4 show clearly that even when alternative measures are used for the base, the rate of citizen complaints in Region East far exceeds the rate for Region West.

OSM's Region East program and personnel were attacked on a variety of fronts. Industry was hostile and suspicious that enforcement was conspiratorily lax in other regions where larger companies mine coal. The states were critical because the federal government had usurped their primary regulatory role, and they feared their "own" coal producers would be disadvantaged by stringent regulation. Moreover, citizens' groups, emboldened and made more determined by passage of SMCRA, were vigilant in their scrutiny of Region East operations. In sum, the political environment in Region East was conflict-ridden, whereas Region

**TABLE 7-4**

**SUMMARY MEASURES OF CITIZEN COMPLAINT ACTIVITY,
JULY 1, 1979, TO JUNE 30, 1980**

| Region | Number of Complaints | Number of Citizen Complaints Per: | | |
|---|---|---|---|---|
| | | Inspector | Inspections | Million Short Tons of Coal |
| East | 445 | 7.42 | 0.67 | 2.35 |
| West | 5 | 0.71 | 0.31 | 0.03 |
| Total (U.S.) | 1043 | 6.56 | 0.61 | 1.28 |

West was much more placid. Of what consequence is this difference in the two regions' political environments?

Reviewing the research literature on regulatory agencies, Thomas suggests that:

> To the extent that an agency must concern itself with a hostile or unpredictable political environment, it will attempt to control the discretion available to officials who must apply rules to individual cases. [1980:121]

Thomas's comment indicates that regulatory agencies might adopt a policelike, impartial enforcement program as a stratagem to separate the agency and its operations from a partisan, conflict-ridden political environment. Along the same lines, an investigator of a legalistic police department claims

> the administrators of these departments want high arrest and ticketing rates [in traffic enforcement] not only because its right but also to reduce the prospect (or the suspicion) of corruption, to protect themselves against criticism that they are not doing their job or are deciding themselves what laws are good or bad, and to achieve, by means of the law, certain larger social objectives. [Wilson, 1968:180]

A similar dynamic occurred in Region East. Little wonder that managers there felt it necessary to "prove" that OSM was not corrupt, playing favorites, or conspiring with large coal producers to destroy their smaller competitors. At the same time, they favored impartial, consistent, nationwide enforcement by OSM. With respect to the more flexible enforcement style adopted in Region West, a Region East manager remarked, perhaps with tongue in cheek, that personnel out there "never read the act."

In the much calmer political environment of Region West, personnel could afford the luxury of more flexible enforcement. Being relatively immune to the suspicions and criticisms of diverse groups, they were less concerned that weak enforcement in other regions would undermine their credibility with Region West operators. Consequently, there was little if any emphasis on the need for nationwide enforcement consistency. It is not surprising, therefore, that the Region West director would say that while the SMCRA

> is a national Act, . . . in fact, there are distinct regions of coal mining with different histories and cultures and, therefore, there

also will be distinct programs implementing this national Act. It isn't a regionalization of the objectives. It's a regionalization of the implementation. [*Energy Daily,* 1978]

There is an additional way in which local conditions in the two regions affected their respective enforcement programs. The mining community in Region West is much smaller and homogeneous than in Region East. Further, mining company representatives with whom regulators interact usually are well-educated and outwardly sympathetic to the goals of regulation. Put another way, the Region West mining community enjoyed a much higher degree of consensus on mining and regulatory objectives than Region East. Wilson has observed that, in communities where there is such substantial consensus, police are likely to

> feel that they can use their judgment in a particular case without having to choose, or without being thought to have chosen, between competing standards of order held by different persons or subcultures. And if the community is small in addition, the police are more likely to have information about the character of a large number of citizens and thus some grounds for making a valid judgment about their likely future conduct. Stated another way, the police in a small town may believe that they are treating equals equally even when they do not treat everybody the same. [1968:219–20]

A final difference in the local environments of regions East and West is paralleled in Wilson's description of legalistic police enforcement:

> [T]he law must be enforced with a special vigor in those areas where community norms appear weakest; failure to do so would penalize law-abiding persons in those areas and inhibit the development of a regard for community norms among the law breakers.[1968:285–86]

Our data suggest that the same relationship is true of regulatory agencies. In the West, where there is a high level of consensus and, presumably, compliance, there is little need for vigorous enforcement. Those already voluntarily in compliance will be relatively unaffected by what happens to those who do not comply. However, in the East, where the rate of compliance is low, regulators must stand ready to employ aggressive enforcement against violators lest the rate erode even further. Strict enforcement serves as a signal of reassurance to voluntary compliers that they will not be harmed economically by their compliance.[2]

# 8  The Agency Under Siege

While regional personnel grappled with the day-to-day problems of implementing the interim regulations, headquarters staff moved ahead with other tasks mandated in the act. They were faced with close deadlines for promulgating permanent regulations and procedures for reviewing them, as well. The agency never had smooth sailing, but now the waters were even more troubled. New attacks were mounted against the OSM, and its broad base of political support was eroding. The changing political context was described by a solicitor:

> It was clear—what—the spring of '78?—that the political acceptability of . . . vigorous . . . implementation of the act . . . was less than wholehearted, both in terms of politicians, as well as in terms of state institutions.

## THE REVOLT OF THE STATES

Since the permanent program regulations were to be the yardstick for evaluating state primacy applications, the states had special reasons to examine critically the agency's openness of the state window, strictures placed on federal grants for the development of state programs, and deadlines imposed by the act. In short order, many of the states grew unhappy with the nature and impact of OSM's programs. By mid-1978 the states began raising the complaints that were to become familiar over the next two years: OSM was arrogant and inflexible in its dealings with the states.

107

There was ample justification for some of these complaints. The OSM had been created to reform the states' programs. It approached the states with the same enforced compliance style that it applied to the coal industry. Many officials of the federal agency were distrustful of the states because of their weak past performances as regulators.

> I think there was a healthy skepticism about the willingness of the states to change direction. And, again, I think if you go and read the legislative history, that attitude existed in Congress.

Some of the states were angered by OSM's enforcement activities under the interim regulatory program. They believed that federal enforcers made them appear incompetent and unwilling to take aggressive enforcement actions.

The states did not speak with one voice; the specific issues that animated individual states varied. As would be expected, there was an East-West split on these issues. For example, western states faced some unique regulatory problems, including special programs for Indian lands, cooperative agreements with the OSM for inspections on federal lands, and OSM's responsibility to review permit applications for mines on federal lands. Our comments are focused on the types of issues that animated most of the states to one degree or another.

Proceeding on three fronts, the states stepped up their attacks after the OSM promulgated its permanent program regulations. First, West Virginia's Governor Jay Rockefeller, at the request of the National Governors' Association, urged Congress to amend the SMCRA. His proposed amendment eventually was added to a Senate bill (S.1403) that was introduced at the behest of the OSM.[1] As amended it required only that state programs be consistent with environmental protection standards contained in the act and not with regulations promulgated by the Office of Surface Mining. The bill was passed by the Senate (U.S. Congress, Senate, 1979), but it did not survive committee review in the House of Representatives. The following year, West Virginia's Senator Robert Byrd used a parliamentary maneuver to attach a similar amendment to a House-passed maritime bill. His effort also failed.[2]

On a second front, state witnesses criticized the OSM in congressional oversight hearings. Wyoming's Governor Edward Herschler took a leading role in these efforts. He told a congressional committee:

> From the beginning the Office of Surface Mining has treated the States as if only the Federal Government could be trusted to care

for the environment. Federal respect for our capabilities has been grudging at best. I think that this attitude is flagrantly contrary to what the Congress intended and that it has engendered a reciprocal mistrust which lies at the heart of the present Federal-State tensions. . . . [T]he Act as passed by Congress is workable. The Office of Surface Mining is not. [U.S. Congress, House, 1979:11]

Charging that OSM demanded state programs to be "clones" of the federal regulatory program, the states balked against regulatory requirements they considered unnecessary or inappropriate. For example, Governor Herschler cited OSM's insistence that Wyoming issue specific regulations for mining by mountaintop removal:

Our Land Quality Division replied that there is no such mining activity in Wyoming and hence such regulation is unnecessary. . . . [OSM's] attorneys responded by saying that "only the future can prove the veracity" of Land Quality's assertion, and that Wyoming must promulgate regulations for mountaintop removal. [U.S. Congress, House, 1979:9]

The states especially resented OSM's insistence that their regulatory programs include specific provisions supported by environmentalists, such as citizen participation in inspection and enforcement and state payment of fees to plaintiffs' attorneys when they sued the state.

Finally, some western governors pressed their complaints about the Office of Surface Mining directly to Department of Interior secretary, Cecil Andrus, a former peer as governor of Idaho. In personal correspondence and in private meetings they castigated the OSM.

During this period of increasing tension between the OSM and the states, the associate solicitor for surface mining issued an opinion on *ex parte* contacts during the rule making (i.e., regulation writing) process. The opinion held that OSM could not meet privately with the states to discuss proposed regulations after the close of the public comment period. Further, meetings held during the public comment period were to be announced in advance and opened to the public. This development severely limited contacts with the states, angered them, and, correctly or not, reinforced their belief that the OSM viewed them as unequal partners, if not adversaries, in the regulatory process.

## THE COAL INDUSTRY'S COUNTERATTACK

The coal industry had subjected the OSM to severe criticism once the final interim regulations were published and federal enforcement began. Throughout the first three years of OSM operations, the coal industry charged that (1) OSM had misinterpreted and exceeded congressional intent, and (2) the regulations did not allow sufficient flexibility in meeting the performance standards in the act and regulations. For example, in comments submitted to the OSM on its proposed permanent regulations, the NCA-AMC Joint Committee charged:

> In all too many caess, the regulations as proposed, are in our opinion, unreasonable and unnecessarily inflexible. In other places, we find that the regulations are in conflict with the legislative intent of the underlying P.L. 95-87, as set forth in its legislative history. [U.S. Congress, Senate, 1979:241]

Acknowledging that the regulations did provide flexibility in some areas, the Joint Committee charged that

> any of the alternatives mentioned could result in enormous economic consequences upon the industry, its customers, and the American consumer as well as resultant impacts upon coal mining communities. [F-507]

Along the same line, MARC complained about the "sheer volume of detailed, technical regulations" contained in the proposed program (F-305).

Appalachian mine opertors charged that the costs of preparing mine permit applications, securing adequate bonds for mining operations, and of designing and building prescribed environmental protection structures was prohibitive. They also claimed that OSM's regulatory program effectively made it impossible for them to mine in many areas of Appalachia and thus denied them their rights to use their land as they saw fit. Put differently, they charged that the federal government was "taking" their property without due process of law. A mine operator who signed his letter "Small Time Operator" wrote to the OSM to complain that the increase in regulation was harming his business.

> I am a small strip-mining coal operator and am very much concerned about the future of our nation. Currently, I have been unable to produce two thousand tons of coal a month. In 1973 I could produce five to six thousand tons a month. . . . I venture to say that ninety percent of these regulations do not relate to the safety and welfare of the people. . . . If there is not some relief of government regulations, a lot of people which are now providing employment trying

to contribute something for the good of our nation will have no
choice but fold. . . . The longer I stay in business, the farther in
the red I have become. I am not a young man and my family's life
savings are invested in this business, but if there is not some relief
from government so more thought can be placed on production, I
along with numerous other small operators will have no choice but
to fall by the wayside. [F-129]

Through their trade association (MARC), these small operators attacked OSM's regulations.

We must . . . strongly re-state our concern for the small operator—
another problem area recognized by Congress but seemingly ignored
by OSM. . . . The permit requirements as defined tend to be what
would normally be needed for a large operation in the west or midwest and have no relevance for small permits in the Appalachian
area. There is no justification for the detailed studies, surveys, and
other requirements on the great majority of smaller permits. To
maintain these detailed requirements will result in the termination
of many of these permits.

Finally, there is absolutely no doubt that the inflationary impact
of these rules as proposed will be staggering. . . . Our preliminary
estimates place the increased cost for mining coal under the Act
from 50% to 100% or more. [F-305]

Attacks on OSM by such operators often were strident.

Large and small coal were united in charging that the federal regulations would increase the cost of mining coal, were responsible for a
sharp decline in coal production at a time when the nation was trying
to achieve energy independence, and were causing unemployment and
operator shutdowns. They pressed these claims at every opportunity and
in every available forum.

The larger coal produceres waged their offensive on a larger number
of fronts. As a regional manager noted:

[In this area] 95 percent of the production is out of the top 100
corporations. Those aren't little mining companies, they're Exxon,
and Shell, and General Dynamics, and Conoco . . . and Ashland
Oil. Hey, *they're* not going to have interference. . . . We were'nt
playing with little wildcat miners in Appalachia. That was a mis-
conception. We're playing with Exxon. We're playing with Shell
Oil, dumping a lot of oil and petroleum profits into coal. They're
playing *high stakes poker.* And they come at you *a lot* of different
ways: better lawyers, lots of Ph.D.s, the political way, . . . the ad
way.

Commencing soon after promulgation of OSM's interim regulations, the coal industry and the states mounted a number of court challenges to the agency's regulatory program. Early in 1978, twenty-two cases involving coal operators, trade associations, and three states came before the U.S. District Court for the District of Columbia (In re Surface Mining Regulation Litigation 452 F. Supp. 327, 1978). The plaintiffs attacked the OSM's interim regulations and asked for summary judgment and a preliminary injunction. The court consolidated the cases.

Industry's challenges alleged both procedural and substantive short-comings in the regulations. The procedural challenges alleged that (1) the Secretary of the Interior failed to consider the effects of regulations on the economy, inflation and the nation's coal supply, and (2) the basis and purpose statement (preamble) that accompanied the regulations was inadequate. The court denied these motions.

The plaintiffs raised nine substantive challenges: (1) five matters slated for regulation in the permanent program were regulated improperly in the interim program, (2) adequate exemption and variance procedures were lacking in the interim regulations, (3) the interim regulations improperly were extended to preexisting structures and facilities, (4) prime farmland standards were improperly extended to nonprime farmland areas, (5) the prime farmlands statutory grandfather exemption was improperly narrowed, (6) waste impoundments (dams) were regulated improperly, (7) the regulations improperly limited the discharge of manganese into alkaline surface waters, and (9) the regulations improperly implemented the act's small operators' exemption. With only three relatively minor exceptions, for which the court remanded the relevant regulations to the secretary for reconsideration, the plaintiffs' motions were denied.

Two other major challenges to the act and to the OSM's interim regulatory program were mounted. The first was brought in the U.S. District Court for the Western District of Virginia. The plaintiffs alleged that provisions of the act that established the interim program violated the commerce clause of the U.S. Constitution. The plaintiffs sought declaratory and injunctive relief. The district court rejected some of the plaintiffs' claims and granted others. The secretary of the interior appealed directly to the U.S. Supreme Court, which merged the case with another one brought by the state of Indiana. On June 15, 1981, the court ruled that Congress, in adopting the act, did not exceed its powers under the commerce clause of the Constitution, nor did the act violate the Fifth and Tenth Amendments to the Constitution (Hodel v. Virginia Surface Mining and Reclamation Assn. 69 L. Ed. 2d).

In 1980, important court decisions were handed down following challenges to various portions of the permanent program regulations. The cases were brought in the U.S. District Court for the District of Columbia (In re Permanent Surface Mining Regulation Litigation, Civil Action #79-1144). Various plaintiffs (including the Pennsylvania Coal Association, the National Coal Association, Peabody Coal Company, the states of Illinois and Virginia, and the National Wildlife Federation) filed nine complaints challenging the permanent regulatory program. the court consolidated the actions and divided the nearly 100 issues into two rounds. The first round issues were dealt with in a February 26, 1980, decision, and the second round was decided on May 16, 1980. The court's opinions upheld the broad powers of the OSM to issue regulations pursuant to the act. However, a number of specific regulations were remanded to the agency for reconsideration because the court found them to be arbitrary, capricious, or inconsistent with the law. In addition, the agency voluntarily remanded a number of its regulations, in part because of court challenges.

According to the National Research Council (1981:97), "certain general points" were decided in these early appellate challenges:

(1) The OSM's authority to promulgate detailed regulations, including design standards, was affirmed.

(2) "Detailed design specifications promulgated for nationwide application . . . can, however, be challenged on technical grounds related to site specific conditions."

(3) Some regulations were challenged successfully on grounds that the agency exceeded its statutory authority. For example, "one court held that since SMCRA requires a 300-ft buffer zone between blasting operations and an occupied dwelling, OSM cannot extend this to a 1,000-ft buffer zone."

(4) "Some of the gaps and overlaps between OSM regulations and those of other regulatory agencies [were] adjusted by court actions."

(5) Exemptions from regulation provided in the SMCRA may not be ignored or circumscribed by the agency.

(6) The agency's jurisdiction over surface disturbances resulting from deep mining was affirmed by the courts.

(7) Direct attacks on the act and the regulations by the states generally failed. The courts found that the states must comply with the act and the agency's regulations, including permitting and bonding.

Understandably, OSM personnel and the agency's solicitors felt vindicated by the court's decision. Regardless of the program's impact on the behavior of mining firms, in the solicitors' eyes it indisputably was successful because it survived litigation almost entirely intact.

The coal industry also mounted a publicity campaign in opposition to the Office of Surface Mining:

> Amax was running full page ads against us, against OSM, in big newspapers. They were running 60-second breaks on prime time TV—Super Bowl halftime, finals of NCAA, World Series. Millions of dollars were spent in advertising contra OSM. . . . Industry spent *a fortune* against this little outfit [OSM].

Although we did not collect data on the industry's media activities, occasionally we saw these media efforts. An examplary ad, paid for by the Mobil Oil Corporation, appeared in the *Washington Star* on February 16, 1981 (p.A-15). Under a bold-type title of "Let's end the coal nightmare," the advertisement responded to "a recent editorial" in the *New York Times,* which asserted editorially that "coal mining in the western United States is not overregulated." The advertisement stated:

> We were so astounded by this statement that we took a closer look at what is required in typical situations by federal and state authorities before a western coal mine can be started.

The ad detailed the alleged complex, time-consuming processes required to secure a permit to mine on federal lands in the West and then concluded:

> The issue isn't *whether* to regulate, but *how.* And finding the kind of regulatory formula that will enable America to put its coal resources to work is more than cosmetic surgery. What is needed, *The Times* notwithstanding is a *major* overhaul, and it's *long* overdue. [emphasis in the original][3]

Not content with the actions described thus far, the coal industries also mounted an intense political attack on the OSM and its operations. Congressional oversight hearings were one battleground. The industry's weapons included support for congressional legislation sharply curtailing the importance of OSM's permanent regulatory program, contacts in the

White House, contacts in the Department of Interior and, finally, nurturance of a coalition with states officials.

Congressional oversight hearings were held in 1979 (both House and Senate committees), 1980 (House), and 1981 (both houses). Excepting the 1981 hearings, which were held after the change in political administrations, the coal industry used these hearings to attack OSM. Generally their complaints were a repetition of those they had made earlier, some as long ago as 1968 when federal legislation first was contemplated: OSM's inflexible regulations, the nation's overriding need for coal energy; the excessive cost of compliance with the regulations; the excessive detail and scope of the regulations; the plight of small coal producers who would be forced out of business because of their inability to comply; OSM's misinterpretation and unreasonable extension of congressional intent; and OSM's deference toward environmentalist groups and sentiments. There was little new in these complaints, but they were repeated in tones of mounting anguish and urgency.

There was one new complaint, however. Industry attacked the agency for its insistence that they and the states meet deadlines established in the act even though OSM had missed some of its deadlines—in the case of the permanent regulations, by several months. This, they charged, was more evidence of the agency's unreasonable, inflexible approach to its mandate and constituencies.

In 1979 congressional testimony, industry was united in requesting two actions. First, they requested an extension of the deadlines required for industry compliance with the regulations and for states' submissions of primacy applications. And second, they supported enactment of S.1403. MARC's president did not mince words in telling the Senate committee:

> I think the only way to solve this problem is to amend the act and amend the act immediately. The public can't wait in gas lines forever. They can't wait another year. The coal operators who are currently marginal are not going to be around next year to wait and see what happens and get more experience.
>
> We have had enough experience. It has been almost 2 years, and everything has been a dismal failure. [U.S. Congress, Senate, 1979:42]

The coal industry also supported attacks on the agency by members of Congress who were angered by "leaked" OSM memoranda. these memos, provided to members of Congress by a disgruntled former OSM employee, became the basis for allegations that the agency was engaged illegally in political lobbying. The same materials proved damaging to the agency also because they contained rather unflattering descriptions of certain members of Congress.

The former employee testified in House oversight hearing during 1979.[4] His testimony lent support to those who had charged for several years that the OSM was staffed by environmental zealots who were determined to punish the coal industry and the states. Along with the "leaked" internal memoranda, the testimony became ammunition for the industry and for members of Congress bent on reshaping the Office of Surface Mining. Because of the materials he provided, the Government Accounting Office (GAO) was asked to determine if OSM officials had engaged in criminal offenses (primarily illegal lobbying). The study produced inconclusive findings and, eventually, the entire incident was permitted to die.

Finally, some of the largest coal producers brought pressure to bear on the Office of Surface Mining through the Department of Energy (DOE) and their contacts in the White House. After the close of the comment period on the proposed permanent regulations, industry representatives approached the DOE, which in turn contacted the President's Council of Economic Advisors (CEA). The CEA then approached the Office of Surface Mining with claims about the inflationary impacts of some of the proposed permanent regulations. CEA requested a meeting with OSM officials to present their materials. OSM refused to meet, citing the fact that the public comment period already had closed. The CEA then approached the Department of Justice which suggested that a meeting would not be improper (i.e., a violation of the Administrative Procedures Act). Consequently, the OSM agreed to hold the meeting, but only with the stipulation that the meeting minutes would be open to the public and that the public comment period would be reopened so that public comments on the CEA materials would be welcome.

The DOE and the CEA primarily expressed concern about one area of the regulations, control of fugitive dust (air quality), which is a "western regulation."

> According to persons who attended the meeting, the council [CEA] officials sought to have one element of the controls deleted as being too expensive; the rule writers contended that the officials' figures were wrong. . . . The council record on the issue, which was made public, was said to be "replete with evidence of solicitation of industry views" by the economic council since the 60-day period for comment on the proposed regulations ended Nov. 27. [Richmond Times-Dispatch, 7 January 1979]

The OSM did not make any substantive changes in the regulations to accommodate the CEA and, ultimately, large coal producers. However, a participant in the meeting said that the OSM almost "was forced to cave in," but managed to avoid doing so when errors were discovered in the CEA's analysis of the regulatory impacts.[5] However, the meetings did force a six-month delay in final publication of the permanent program regulations, and this, of course, set back even further the original timetable for state program submission and implementation.

## THE STATES-INDUSTRY COALITION

The states and the coal industry voiced a number of virtually identical complaints about the Office of Surface Mining, its regulations and its operations. They charged that the agency viewed them as adversaries or incompetents who could not be trusted to establish and implement credible reclamation programs without close federal oversight. By 1979 the coal industry began to sound like rock-ribbed defenders of states' rights in their complaints about the Office of Surface Mining. More specifically, industry supported passage of S.1403 and joined with the states in a number of court challenges to the act and regulations.

Finally, both groups, in 1979, began to sound the same theme about the dangers of federal bureaucratization. They charged that the Office of Surface Mining, following some immutable law of bureaucracy, was bent on expanding its payroll and responsibilities. Complaining about federal "redtape," Governor Herschler told a congressional committee:

> Since a great deal of this redtape ultimately has little to do with the welfare of the land, it seems sensible to conclude that it is related to the welfare of OSM instead. It is inevitable that this redtape will be used to justify additional redtape, and additional OSM. . . . We should stop this bureaucratic juggernaut before it grows beyond all control. [U.S. Congress, Senate, 1979:10]

A reading of congressional oversight transcripts suggests that both the states and the coal industries wanted to remove all threat of future problems from OSM by severe cuts and alterations in its budget and organizational structure. Only through a radical transformation of the agency could they be certain of no further interference.

## "FRIENDLY" SNIPING BY ENVIRONMENTALISTS

Individuals and organizations in the environmentalist community were not idle during this period when OSM came under attack from industry and the states. Determined to prevent any slippage of agency resolve to implement a tough regulatory program, they maintained a watchful eye on the agency. The Council of the Southern Mountains brought suit against the agency for failure to carry out the required number of inspections mandated in the act (Council of the Southern Moutains v. Andrus, U.S. District Court, D.C., Civil Action #79-1521, 1980). Acknowledging its failure, the agency settled out of court with a written promise to fulfill the mandate.

Environmentalist groups employed litigation for three principal reasons: (1) to win court decisions in order to maintain and to buttress the stringency of the OSM regulatory program and operations; (2) to protect, if not enlarge, opportunities for citizen participation in many administrative procedures connected with implementation of federal and state surface mining programs; and (3) in the words of one of the OSM's headquarters executives, "to fire at the industry."

## RELATIONS WITH THE REGIONAL OFFICES

Some aspects of relations between OSM headquarters and the regional offices duplicated, at a much lower level of intensity, but for substantially the same reasons, relations between OSM and the states.

> [T]he regional OSM people—there would be a spectrum—were more eager to accommodate either the states' views or the industry's views than the Solicitor's Office, or even possibly OSM in Washington were prepared to do—which is natural; the field is always gonna be that way.

The result was a tendency to discount feedback grounded in the firsthand experience and concerns of the field-level regulatory staff.

> Some of the folks at headquarters were not "field-oriented." Of course, they were giving their full time to regulation writing; that was driving headquarters. . . . They were doing it pretty much in a vacuum. . . . The regional directors, who constitute the senior staff . . . were never consulted. The regional directors had no input into the regulations. . . . [A]t that point, we were . . . preoccupied

with implementing the interim program, and hiring people, [and opening field offices].

As the target date for publication of the permanent program regulations drew near, regional managers grew increasingly apprehensive, based on the draft they had seen, about their field-level reception. Largely on their own initiative, the five regional directors requested a meeting with headquarters managers to discuss the substance and potential impact of the forthcoming regulations.

> The regulations . . . were exceedingly burdensome in terms of just the detail and . . . it was just overdone. There's no questions about that. . . . We felt, meaning all the regional directors, that these things were just too comprehensive, and too all-encompassing, too detailed. And we're gonna get killed—"we," the agency, "we," the program.

The regional directors arrived in Washington and were given a short time to examine the package of regulations. Dismayed with what even a cursory review revealed, they elected a spokesperson to meet with headquarters managers the following day to press their concerns. Despite the expression of concern by the regional directors, "nothing happened, nothing changed."[6]

## AGENCY IMPACTS

The barrage of attacks to which the Office of Surface Mining was subjected during 1978–1980 was not without impact. To be sure, it is not always easy to distinguish these effects from those occasioned or made possible merely by the fact that the agency, at least by mid-1979, had completed some of the most pressing objectives (promulgation of the interim and permanent program regulations). Now there was time to review agency operations. Some changes were fundamental and suggested that prior to the 1980 presidential elections there was a gradual "softening" of the stringent policies OSM pursued initially.

### Operational Consequences

From the outset, OSM adopted a highly centralized, attorney-driven mode of operation. This operating dynamic dominated the agency during its first year of operation. It enabled the agency to accomplish a prodigious amount of work in a short period of time. But the agency paid a price for its effectiveness: its legalistic style severely exacerbated worsening relations with the states.

The Department of Interior's associate solicitor for surface mining came to be a lightning rod for the states' attacks on the Office of Surface Mining. Individually and through the Interstate Mining Compact Commission, they urged Secretary Andrus to dismiss him. In mid-1979 they prevailed.[7] Agency personnel viewed the move as "political." A respondent told us, simply, that it became necessary for "someone to fall on their sword." As if to make sure the states were aware of the new signals from Washington, a few weeks later the Department of Interior moved to revise the earlier restrictions on *ex parte* contacts with the states (*Federal Register* 44[19 September 1979]:54444).

### Regulatory "Softening"

Early in 1979, one of the first permit applications for a new, large, western mine was sent to Washington for final decision by Secretary Andrus. The planned mine, a joint venture by two large corporations, would be located on Indian lands. Believing that revegetation potentially could be very difficult to achieve on the mine site, OSM's Region V personnel recommended a limited—seven years—approval of the mine permit. At the end of that time, the mine operators would have to demonstrate that revegetation had been accomplished before mining could continue. Officials in the Department of Interior were subjected to pressures from the tribe, the states, and from politicians to grant a full permit. The Department of Interior established a special technical panel to review the permit application and countermanded the regional recommendation. Not only was the permit granted for a longer period of time, but the permit conditions imposed upon *the OSM* the obligation to demonstrate that revegetation *cannot* succeed before a permit extension can be denied. This action was viewed by some in Region V as evidence that the agency (or, at least, officials in the Department of Interior) was willing to compromise and soften the stringent permitting requirements of the regulatory program.

### Regional Feedback

By 1980 the regional offices were busily engaged in review of state submissions for regulatory primacy. As a result of these experiences and partly because the regions were in close contact with the states, the regional offices began to provide Washington with feedback on state-federal relations.

> [T]hings [were] filtering from the regional staff up to the Washington leadership. We saw that the regional staff said, felt, that [the regulations] had very little flexibility and insisted on, practically word for word, correspondence. And then as the Washington staff learned that that might not be very reasonable, we were able to step back a little bit. But it had to be done pretty much at the top level, because of the impression those people had that it came from there.

For a variety of reasons, then, some of the headquarters executives, by 1980, began to see and appreciate the limitations of their individual and collective regulatory approach.

> [A]s we got in '80, and decisions on the state programs . . . we saw more flexibility, not a *lot,* I don't think but it was certainly starting to come out. Then, as we talked to specific states about the detailed regulations which they had, ones which didn't follow the federal regulations very closely, we got to appreciate more and more the problems which they had, and took different approaches—and approved them. Montana was the first state, in the spring of '80, to come in and really make a hard pitch to do things their way on a relatively small number of items. . . . In some cases they had real differences of approach. And they wanted to maintain them. And after a *hard* negotiating session between [OSM HQ personnel and state staffs], we ended up accepting most of what they wanted to do. Then, as a few other states got into the same position, we came to be able to do that more and more.

There is no doubt that political attacks on the agency played a part in this move toward a more conciliatory stance with the states. One respondent told us baldly: "I think S.1403 scared us quite a bit. We hadn't realized the *depth* of feeling that was out there." He also said:

> I think there was an attitude in-house that went something like this: We kept saying to the states: "Propose some differences, and a lot of them will be acceptable. If you follow the general procedures, and propose something different, we'll consider it. And if it's good, we'll *approve* it." . . . What we didn't see was that the states were in *no mood* to deal with us in that fashion."

Sensing perhaps that the federal government really did not want to regulate its large number of mines, Kentucky virtually threatened to make them do so, by refusing to submit a revised primacy application. Its thinly-veiled threat produced a real fear in Washington, and it helped some headquarters executives see the desirability of a more conciliatory stance toward the states.

The agency believed that legislative efforts to curb their powers (such as S.1403) might be defeated if they could gain some allies in the states. A more flexible approach to the review of state programs helped in this regard. In addition, the agency sent special emissaries to confer with and to reassure at least one of their most vocal critics. All these efforts met with some success; eventually some of the western states publicly opposed legislation to trim the agency's sails.

By late 1980, there was a perceptible, although not a major, shift occurring in the shared understanding of headquarters personnel regarding the agency's mission and strategies for pursuing it. At one of the regular meetings of regional and headquarters executives, there was an indication that headquarters would welcome a move toward more flexible regulations. Little came of this, however, since the meeting occurred less than one month before the 1980 presidential election.

## IMPLICATIONS

From its origins, the Office of Surface Mining took an adversarial stance toward the coal industry and the states. Both were viewed as in need of substantial reform. Since neither was trustworthy, negotiated compliance was eschewed. The OSM was attempting to override the states' rights component of the act. Congress had been unable to resolve the issue of the degree of federal regulatory control over state programs. In effect they dumped the problem on the bureaucrats. When the states revolted against the federal state managers' actions, they found allies in congress and in the coal industry. The states accomplished what the coal industry had not been able to do. They got the federal agency's attention and, eventually, forced openings toward negotiated complaince. There is a fundamental lesson here: local state agencies serve as a proxy for capital in their battle against relatively autonomous federal-level state managers. Local state managers are more responsive to economic conditions than are federal-level state managers. In revolting against the OSM, local state managers were not acting as instruments of capital, they were simply doing their job, "steering" the local economy by promoting a good business climate.

# 9 A Theoretical Reprise

In previous chapters, we have presented a detailed narrative development of a new federal regulatory agency. Our examination of the stages of the regulatory process in the Office of Surface Mining has been guided by ideas and explanations drawn from diverse theories of the state and by our typology of regulatory styles. In this chapter, we reappraise our findings. First, we examine the goodness of fit between our data and the three forms of state theory presented in chapter 1. Our synthetic interpretation stresses the centrality of state managers in the regulatory process. Second, we review the determinants of the rather extreme enforced compliance style that characterized the Office of Surface Mining. Third, we analyze the costs and benefits of this style. Finally, we present some policy implications we have drawn from our findings.

## THE REGULATION OF SURFACE MINING IN THE LIGHT OF THEORIES OF THE STATE

How did it happen that in 1977, some fifteen years after the beginning of the rapid growth of strip mining, the federal government became involved in intricate regulation of the mining process?

The coal industry is internally and externally competitive: internally competitive because the supply is great and ownership is not concentrated; externally competitive because the demand for coal is elastic, substitute fuels being available. Regulation of such a competitive industry is costly to the producers. It is doubtful that the full cost can be passed on to the consumer. Thus, the new law (Surface Mining Control and Reclamation Act of 1977) had the potential of depressing profits and driving some marginal operators from the field.[1] More importantly, the law was viewed by coal operators as a massive violation of their right to control the production process. In short, the coal companies fought the law vigorously. They were able to delay the passage of the bill and won *some* compromises, but the ferocity of their opposition was partially responsible for the law's detail and stringency.

The regulation of surface mining forced firms to internalize production costs borne previously by residents of mining areas. Although a small core of politicians fought long and hard for the bill, it would be a mistake to view it simply as an invention of state managers. Like other corporate reform laws, it was a product of long years of struggle by a handful of professional reformers who mobilized a social movement supported by constituents not directly harmed by surface mining problems.

Still, law on the books means little in and of itself. Law acquires direction, purpose, and substance through the actions of enforcement bureaucracies and personnel. Refashioned now as "law as social action," it constrains behavior.

The new act produced an administrative organization that consisted mostly of career bureaucrats, not of rabid environmentalists. However, a handful of top managers were strong proponents of strict autonomy from the agency's coal-producing clientele. They generated an organizational culture, characterized by high morale and a strong sense of purpose, that focused on strictly enforced compliance with the law.

The new OSM administrative bureaucracy then operationalized the law into rules. Paying heed to suggestions of environmentalists and ignoring the coal industry, the OSM's managers produced a rigorous, detailed set of regulations. These regulations, especially those with strict design standards, took the industry by surprise, and they reacted vigorously. They took their case to the courts, but found little relief.

Still, a rule on the books means little if not enforced. In practice, implementation of enforcement varied by region. The effect was that the new act was not enforced to the letter, as evidenced by the failures of OSM regional offices to inspect all mining operations and to impose penalties for violations. Still, the new OSM regulated surface mining much more rigorously than the states. For this reason, it was exceedingly unpopular in the coal fields. There is little doubt that the quality of the environment was enhanced. Disagreement remains over whether the price was excessive.

As previously indicated, one of our central purposes is to explore the extent to which certain developments in neo-Marxist theories of the state are more promising than others in explaining social regulation. At least for the early years of federal surface mining regultion, the strong form of special interest theories (capture instumentalism, and corporate liberalism) seems to have almost no bearing on explaining what happened. There is nothing in our data that indicates the act was a consequence of efforts by enlightened coporate liberals to dampen competition or to control markets. It might even be said that there are *no* enlightened corporate liberals in the coal industry.

The explanatory relevance of the weak forms of special interest theory can be seen in the conflict and compromise in the making of the law. Environmental movement organizations influenced the making of the regulations. Under certain macroeconomic conditions (relative economic growth), noncapitalist, if not anticapitalist class forces, can be mobilized effectively to expand state control of productive processes. It remains to be seen whether this control is more than symbolic or temporary.

The OSM's initial regulations and enforcement procedures indicate clearly that its state managers were relatively autonomous from capital and from Congress. It is the task of state managers, as a whole, to steer the system. Functionalist forms of neo-Marxism stress the role of the state (thus, of its managers) in rationalizing the economy, the emphasis here being on promoting capital accumulation. A second major function of the state is the enlistment of support, in the form of self-legitimation of the state itself and legitimation of the economic system. Formally, surface mining regulation, like social regulation in general, represents a rationalization of the economic system. It entails the internalization by firms of costs that previously had been dumped on external parties. However, this economic rationalization is detrimental to profit accumulation for the affected fraction of captial. Therefore, since coal is a widely used captial resource, it does not seem likely that consequent increases in the costs of coal production are beneficial to capital as a whole. Rather, the regulation of surface mining is an instance of action by state managers to legitimate the state as the representative of the "public interest" in controlling corporate wrongdoing. In legitimizing itself, the state also legitimized the economic system by providing the appearance that capital is subject to popular control.

These managers did not see themselves as agents of a class struggle against the hated capitalists, but they did distrust the coal industry enough to want to keep them at arm's length. Although they engaged in class struggle, they did so in the name of the public interest and bureaucratic integrity.

The passage of the federal law was a step toward rationalization of the economy in a second sense. It was the weakness of the state laws, coupled with lax enforcement, that stimulated the movement for a federal law. A stringent national law, meant to be uniformly applied across the coal-producing states, replaced a set of state laws that varied considerably in quality and level of enforcement.

None of the theories of the state provide much help in understanding the role of the local states in the political economy of a federal system, but considerable light can be thrown on the matter by drawing on world systems theory (Wallerstein, 1979). World systems theory transforms the traditional Marxist analysis of class struggle between capitalists and workers within nations into an analysis of struggle between (as well as across) states or regions. Core states (regions) represent the interests of international capital in exploiting the labor power and resources of peripheral states (regions). Peripheral areas must compete in a world market for capital and sales. In the United States, coal is generally found only in peripheral areas. America's coal fields are peripheral not only in the sense that they are off the beaten path, but also to the extent that they are resource export economies. Since the coal is absentee owned, these areas are also capital export economies. Not only coal, but profits flow out. Thus, they are underdeveloped areas. Since the coal supply is ample and the industry is competitive and since the areas are dependent on the coal industry for employment (including petty bourgeois leasing operations) and tax revenue, regional governments (the local states) are structurally constrained to act as capitalists and to compete with each other for sales. These structural constraints militate against strict regulation.

Under these conditions, the passage of a federal law to eliminate externalities may be viewed as a step toward resolution of environmental crises and rationalization of the economy by national state managers. However, local state managers are responsible for steering their local economies, and because they desired to retain their limited autonomy, they fought to retain some element of local control. As a result, the new surface mining act carried an ambiguous message. On one hand, it espoused national regulatory standards, but, on the other hand, it mandated the quick return to the states of enforcement rights.

This ambiguity had important consequences. In the short run, the local state managers, rather than the corporations, took the lead in fighting the federal program. In the long run, the combination of a captured federal agency and the structural constraints on local enforcement surely will lead to a marked decline in rigorous enforcement.

## TOWARD A CLARIFICATION OF STATE THEORY

There are a variety of complex, often contradictory, neo-Marxist theories of the state. The application of neo-Marxist theories of the state to our study of surface mining regulation points to the need for greater theoretical clarity, particularly in the specification of explanatory mechanisms—that is, of the means by which state policy is established. To the extent that these theories are falsifiable, they must be tested and reformulated in the light of disciplined data collection and analysis. Thus, we need more research on the formation of laws that criminalize corporate behavior and more studies of actual enforcement policies. Our research suggests the need to incorporate several elements into neo-Marxist theories of the state: (1) interest groups and social movements as organizational mechanisms through which resources are mobilized for class struggle; (2) the role of state managers both in representing and controlling capital; (3) the role of local state managers and their relationship to national state managers (the dialectic of federalism); (4) the process by which economic conditions constrain policy formation; and (5) the relative autonomy of law as a constraint on policy.

These mechanisms are means by which the state adapts the capitalist system to historically specific conditions. The introduction of these elements does not damage the basic argument of neo-Marxist theory that the state is a capitalist state. The state remains a capitalist state because it must promote economic growth and accumulation. This is so because the state is dependent on growth for its resources and legitimation.

## REGULATORY STYLES AND STRATEGIC OPTIONS[2]

We have stressed the centrality of state managers in state policy formation and implementation. We believe that our data on the Office of Surface Mining best fit the intermediate forms of special interest theory, most particularly the neo-Marxist post-structural version. OSM's managers were constrained by a number of conditions and processes, but they were relatively autonomous in their selection of strategies that defined a particular organizational style. The managers of the Office of Surface Mining, from its inception until its takeover by Reagan administration appointees, adopted an enforced compliance style at almost every step in the regulatory process. This style may be contrasted with its polar opposite: negotiated compliance. Both styles are intended to induce firms' compliance through the application of a given set of statutes and administrative rules.

A negotiational style promotes compliance through a flexible, situationally attuned administrative process in which the mechanisms for attaining compliance are only loosely constrained. Such a style may reflect a strategic plan, or it may emerge incrementally. Old-style regulatory agencies generally followed a negotiated compliance model. For that reason, they were often criticized for being too flexible and too accommodative toward industry, features that presumably facilitate capture (Bernstein, 1955; Friendly, 1962). An enforced compliance style promotes compliance through a fully rationalized system of justice; that is, a system in which both the goals of the system and the means of attainment are clearly specified and tightly connected. An enforced compliance style is almost always the consequence of a strategic plan.

Relatively formal rule-making procedures are required by statute. These rule-bound procedures imply a built-in adversarial structure that encourages control by legal experts. The OSM's rule-making process had an adversarial quality that extended beyond these strictures. Comments from the coal industry were viewed with strong skepticism, and contacts with industry were avoided. The production of the regulations was dominated by an emphasis on comprehensive, detailed, and legally defensible rules.

Consequently, the regulations reflected a legalistic rather than a discretionary orientation toward the enabling statute and toward the activities to be controlled. The intent was to eliminate ambiguity concerning what was necessary for compliance (cf. National Research Council, 1981a:37–43). Although the regulations did include some discretionary elements, nearly always these were specified by the act or by subsequent judicial decisions. Moreover, the new OSM incorporated enforced compliance assumptions into the regulations, including promulgation of design criteria.

In our ideal-typical model of the enforced compliance style, we presumed it would be characterized by a centralized organization and tight coupling to local state agencies. The OSM did not fit this pattern. Although implementation nominally was decentralized through five regional offices, strict rule application was the accepted norm, excepting Region West. Moreover, the federal agency was loosely and ambiguously coupled to local state agencies. Nevertheless, state agencies were treated as though they were tightly coupled to the Office of Surface Mining, since they were dependent on it for approval of their regulatory programs. In short, in spite of the formal structure, the OSM took a strong enforced compliance stance regarding state primacy. The OSM exacerbated the problem by its policy of limiting communications with the local states. The ambiguous structural relationship between the OSM and the local states opened the door to demands by the states for negotiated compliance policies.

The OSM's implementation of the interim program was stringent by intent. Exercise of interpretive discretion by field-level personnel was limited. Inspectors were told to "go by the book," and accommodative negotiation with operators was discouraged. An enforced compliance style was evident in the agency's centralized assessment of fines. This mode of assessment was an attempt to eliminate discretion and negotiation in sanctioning. In the application of sanctions, however, the agency's performance fell short of headquarters executives' original expectations. Fines were modest in amount and collection was ineffective. The widespread reduction or elimination of fines as a reward for the abatement of violations reflected an accommodative orientation; many times, fines were renegotiated in conference hearings.

## DETERMINANTS OF THE OSM'S REGULATORY STYLE

What accounts for the pervasiveness of the enforced compliance style in the early days at the Office of Surface Mining? Certainly each selection of an enforced compliance option generated a new set of constrainsts, both on the coal industry and on the agency itself. Avoidance of negotiation in the rule-making process helped generate a legalistic, detailed set of regulations. These rules, in turn, encouraged stringent implementation. The agency's strategic choices were determined by its guiding ideology, but also by a set of external constraints.

### The Guiding Ideology

The basic options facing the OSM were specified by a former official of the Department of the Interior:

> There are two ways of going. You can implement a regulatory program slowly, by committees, clawing, fighting, pushing all the way. Or, you can do the whole thing and spend your time in a more controlled retreat, defending what you've done, as opposed to continually trying to create.

The agency opted for "doing the whole thing." Fully believing that the two enforcement styles were variants of *one* process, its executives determined that the best way to guard against an early drift toward negotiational strategies was to begin operations at other extreme. In the words of a solicitor, "Wherever there was a chance to implement *more* as opposed to *less,* they did it."

Policy choices often reflect the underlying values and, at times, the ideologies of particular groups or classes. One such ideology, reformism, was a powerful determinant of the enforced compliance style that shaped the regulatory process during the OSM's initial period.[3] *Reformism* is a set of ideas reflecting the interests of the "new class" (the upper-middle class of highly-educated, professional employees).[4] A central component of reformism is the idea that social problems can be resolved and the public interest best served through the critical application of knowledge by autonomous experts. Reformism is characterized by a pervasive distrust of business and by a basic suspicion of any state or federal agency that seems to have been, or is likely to be, captured by industry.

The rule of law is one of the few mechanisms available for institutionalizing such misgivings. Accordingly, the whole thrust of the OSM's regulatory program may be interpreted as the use of law to maintain the separation of industry and state in the regulatory process. It was assumed that truly autonomous regulation could be maintained only through the development and application of the rule of law at every point. This ideology was not ever fully articulated within the agency. Yet most agency personnel from headquarters to the field believed that the coal industry should be strictly controlled by autonomous experts through the rule of law and mechanisms of enforced compliance.

The guiding ideology was widely accepted in the Washington office and in the Appalachian regions. It was largely rejected by the Region West director. As might be expected, reformism was more characteristic of inspection and enforcement personnel than of others. The early recruits to the agency were more committed to the guiding ideology than the later ones. Throughout the agency, commitment to the guiding ideology eroded with time and experience.

## Statutory Constraints

For any regulatory agency, a major determinant of compliance strategies is the language of the enabling legislation itself. Capture theories generally suggest that weak forms of regulation flow from discretionary and accommodative policies, which result from intended vagueness and ambiguities in the legislative mandate (Kolko, 1965; Weinstein, 1968). In direct response to such theories, the establishment of the new regulatory agencies was increasingly based on tighter, more specific legislation (Marcus, 1980).

The legislative mandate for the creation of the Office of Surface Mining was especially detailed and precise, even in comparison with the legislated mission of other new regulatory agencies (e.g., EPA, OSHA). The Surface Mining Control and Reclamation Act included 115 environmental performance standards and placed very stringent deadlines on the agency and the states. The specificity of the legislative mandate placed strong constraints on the subsequent development of the regulatory program, enabling (if not forcing) the OSM to select legalistic enforced compliance strategies. Furthermore, the deadlines imposed by the law were important constraints in shaping such strategies.

When asked to discuss the agency's mission or mandate, OSM officials typically replied that it was simply to implement the law: "Our priorities were pretty well established by the Act." "You just have to read section I of the act, and it's a pretty clear statement of the mission of the agency." Clearly discussion of options revolved around *narrow issues,* not around the basic direction of the agency.

Public Law 95–87 contains numerous ambiguous details, but its listing of thirteen purposes clearly indicates that it was intended as a rigorous environmental protection law. For example, section 102.(c) states the law was enacted to "assure that surface mining operations are not conducted where reclamation as required by this Act is not feasible."

Enabling legislation for many regulatory agencies does not clearly specify "firm choices between regulatory effectiveness and economic continuity" (Kagan, 1978:66). The SMCRA makes a ritualistic bow toward assuring "that the coal supply essential to the Nation's energy requirement . . . is provided" and that a balance is struck "between protection of the environment and agricultural productivity and the Nation's need for coal" (section 102.[f]). Significantly, however, the act mentions only that the *underground* coal mining industry is "essential to the national interest" (section 101.[b]). The act is silent on ensuring a balance of environmental protection and surface mining development. The legal mandate for strong deterrence of environmental degradation is clear. The agency accepted this mandate as its beacon.

Nevertheless, at least two broad mandates of the act clearly failed to constrain the direction taken by the initial leadership at the OSM. First, the relationship between the agency and the states is left quite ambiguous by the act. On the one hand, a stated purpose of the act is to "assist the states in developing and implementing a program to achieve the purposes of this Act" (section 102.[g]). On the other hand, the act strongly implies a more authoritative role for the OSM in relation to state programs when it mandates the agency to "establish a nationwide program" (section 102.[a]). Based on an interpretation of strong federal priority, the agency applied its enforced compliance style to the states, and this strategy caused major problems for the developing program. Second, the opening section on environmental protection standards indicates that regulations "shall be concise and written in plain, understandable language" (section 501.[a]). The bulky packages of complicated regulations produced by the agency did not meet this requirement.

## Political Constraints

The Office of Surface Mining operated in a political environment that generated major constraints on the development of discretionary, negotiated compliance policies. Kagan's review of, previous research on regulatory agencies concludes that:

> [A] regulatory program which experiences high public visibility, which is subject to objective measures of performance, which is confronted with a more balanced pressure group structure, and which has multiple sources of intelligence and advice, is more likely to maintain a relatively stringent stance. [1978:68]

All these determining conditions apply to the OSM. Forced to develop its regulation program on the periphery of a highly charged political arena, the agency remained publicly visible due to continuing oversight by concerned interest groups. The agency was never enmeshed in the traditional "iron triangle" (agency, regulated industry and congressional committee) of capture (Weaver, 1978). Rather, it was forced to deal with a shifting balance of conflicting interests: environmentalists, large coal, small coal, the states, Congress, and the courts.

Having lost the battle for abolition of strip mining, environmentalists and citizens' groups pressured the agency toward the most stringent implementation possible. They had considerable influence in shaping OSM policies because they knew the law and contributed strong legal defenses for their suggested wording of the regulations.

Having lost the battle for complete freedom from federal regulation, the coal industry pressed for flexible rules and lenient enforcement. Even though the industry produced extensive technical comments on the proposed regulations, relatively few revisions were triggered thereby. Industry's position was adopted only when it stood on firm legal ground. The coal industry had little success in setting limitations on the directions taken by the OSM during the Carter administration. When it lost the struggle for general, discretionary rules, the industry carried its fight to the courts and to the states. Small coal operators, who were more seriously affected by the new regulations than large coal companies, fought the agency tooth and nail. Their truculence only rigidified the agency's position.

Public Law 95-87 was a product of state regulatory failure. Thus, the intent of the act, whatever its formal obeisance to states' rights, was to compel compliance with its purposes. The states fought for relative autonomy from federal control, for greater flexibility and accommodation in formulating regulations, and for negotiation between state and federal technical experts. States' opposition to OSM was based on a desire to adapt the regulations to differing geologic and climatic conditions, to maintain their autonomy and self-respect, and to protect their local industry.

Congress, which had remained on the sidelines during the first two years of the OSM's life, was enlisted on the side of the states in 1979. When a bill that would have curtailed the agency's power over state primacy (S.1403) passed the Senate by a substantial majority, it was clear that the agency's enforcement mandate had been seriously eroded. By failing to negotiate with the states and by neglecting lines of communication with Congress, the agency overplayed its hand. Then OSM leaders felt constrained to take a more conciliatory stance in negotiating primacy and cooperative agreements with the states.

Finally, the courts were an important force in the politics of surface mining regulation. The major battles over the implementation of regulations occurred with the threat of litigation in mind. Challenges to more than 100 OSM regulations were brought in court, including important constitutional issues (Hodel v. Virginia Surface Mining and Reclamation Assn., 1971, 69 L. Ed. 2d). In response to such litigation, the Office of Surface Mining oriented its actions toward legal defensibility. Thus, a program that was based on a stringent law and an adversarial reformist ideology took a further legalistic turn. Because the actions of the Office of Surface Mining were successfully defended in the vast majority of these cases, the courts were a major ally in the agency's quest for autonomy. Anticipatory response to judicial decisions was a key factor in establishing the enforced compliance style throughout the agency.

## The State of the Economy

State managers, both elected and appointed, are necessarily constrained by "business confidence" (Block, 1977). Most of the new social regulatory agencies were established in the relatively prosperous economic climate of the early 1970s. Two earlier versions of the SMCRA were thwarted by presidential veto. Nevertheless, the strong enforced compliance mandate of the act reflected congressional optimism about the state of the economy. As the economy and business confidence declined during the late 1970s, the OSM felt increased pressure to relax its policies and to expand its negotiations with the states. Thus, even before the change in presidential admisistrations, the agency was moving toward negotiated compliance policies on several fronts.

### Resource Constraints

An inadequate budget is an obvious constraint on agency effectiveness and a basis for capture. Lack of start-up funds undoubtedly increased the influence of Department of Interior solicitors in shaping the direction taken by the agency. In this instance, the resource squeeze enhanced the power of those most fearful of capture. Later, insufficient resources for inspections did not seem to affect basic policy in any significant way. However, lack of funds seriously limited the agency's ability to assess and collect fines.

Another resource constraint conducive to capture is lack of skilled experts in the area to be regulated (Mitnick, 1980). In formulating and implementing their programs, many agencies have been dependent on industry expertise. In contrast to many captured agencies (Mitnick, 1980), OSM did not rely on the regulated industry for basic information or for personnel. Office of Surface Mining employees were prohibited, by the SMCRA, from having any financial interest in coal mining. Nor did the agency attempt to recruit staff with backgrounds in the coal industry. Moreover, we discovered few instances of career mobility from agency to the regulated industry. The absence of such personnel interchange was an intended constraint on negotiated compliance strategies. From the standpoint of the coal industry, the resulting lack of expertise was a major source of "bad" regulation (i.e., technically incompetent and unnecessarily restrictive). However, the OSM was able to draw from other federal agencies a wide range of technical experts on mining and the environment. Thus, agency officials were satisfied with the technical quality of their personnel on the task force, in headquarters, and in the regions.

The most common internal criticisms of the hierarchy at OSM and in the Department of Interior were a pervasive absence of political and communicative skills and poor coordination of implementation from the

Washington office. These human capital shortcomings helped to shape the directions taken by the agency. When leadership positions were filled by administrative and legal activists, the agency failed to seek the political support needed for the emerging controversial program. In the eyes of some OSM executives, rising opposition to the stringent program could have been stifled by better communications with congressional supporters, the White House, and state governors. In the view of others, such political groundwork would have set limits on the development of a stringent program by revealing its lack of support.

Finally, the availability of time may shape regulatory policy. Earlier we pointed out that numerous legislated deadlines were placed on OSM and state operations. The significance of these deadlines in constraining policy options cannot be exaggerated. Tight "agency-forcing" (Ackerman and Hassler, 1981) limited the possibility of amicable negotiations with the industry and the states. The time factor probably increased the power of the legal staff in rule making and likely contributed to the enforced compliance style that permeated the surface mining regulations. In addition, time constraints on the promulgation of regulations exacerbated the isolation of headquarters staff from the regions and the states. No doubt time limitations were a definite factor in the choice of a stringent, rather than an accommodative, implementation policy. In the words of an OSM headquarters executive:

> [The] states at that time were soon to be submitting their state programs, so it looked like the interim program would—a year or so later—be out of existence. [We thought it] was rather absurd to start an educational type of enforcement policy for the short remaining interim program period. . . . We just felt there wasn't enough time to give a lot of first bites out of the apple to [coal] operators.

## AN EVALUATION OF ENFORCED COMPLIANCE

Regulatory policies may be examined in terms of manifest and latent consequences for the larger goals of the agency. OSM's goals were the deterrence of environmentally-damaging surface mining activities, the assurance of compliance with requirements of the SMCRA, and the establishment of regulatory autonomy. Next we summarize some of the benefits of the OSM enforced compliance policies and examine their costs. We present propositional statements, which are hypotheses subject to further testing in comparative studies of the regulatory process, particularly in new-style agencies.

## Benefits of Enforced Compliance

(1) An enforced compliance strategy is a *relatively efficient basis for getting a program started.* Through the early establishment of specific goals, an agency is able to avoid delay stemming from internal negotiations concerning its mission. In addition, an enforced compliance strategy limits the extent and duration of external bargaining and narrowly specifies the issues open to negotiation. For the Office of Surface Mining, the deadlines mandated by statute and the lack of fiscal resources produced massive confusion. The building of a new agency and the writing of new regulations require extensive internal negotiation over an endless array of details. Given the time constraints, the agency was forced to limit the discussion of options. In the eyes of its top administrators, the agency had no basic alternatives; it did what it had to do to get the show on the road. By limiting negotiation, the OSM was able to avoid the lengthy delays that had characterized rule making and implementation by the Environmental Protection Agency (Marcus, 1980).

(2) An enforced compliance strategy *maximizes immediate compliance.* Negotiation in the agency's formulation of detailed rules and precise standards was strictly limited. The sudden introduction of enforced compliance is a form of shock treatment. It lets the regulated party know that an agency is serious, tough, honest, and efficient. OSM field inspectors were instructed to enforce the regulations to the letter. Fines were meant to be stringent and immediate. There can be little doubt that the OSM's enforced compliance strategy was immediately effective in limiting environmental damage. Field-level inspectors we interviewed were nearly unanimous in their belief in the efficacy of their actions. Perhaps more impressive testimony came from our interviews with coal operators, whose complaints against the OSM never included the belief that the new federal enforcement actually increased environmental damage.

(3) An enforced compliance strategy *provides a strong defense against litigation.* By promulgating and implementing a stringent set of rules, the Office of Surface Mining avoided litigation from environmentalists. Massive litigation against the EPA and the OSHA (Marcus, 1980; Kelman, 1980) gave the OSM every reason to believe that they also would face such tests. The OSM's solicitors were aware that a detailed record of correct procedures provides

an excellent legal basis for regulatory policies. In the large number of cases brought by the coal industry, the agency generally was successful in defending its policies. Careful legal construction of the rules and enforcement policies generally paid off in later court battles. In the case of the environmentalist complaint against failure to carry out the required number of mandated inspections, the agency settled out of court by pledging to fulfill the law.

(4) The institution of a stringent set of rules and enforcement policies *provides an agency with a strong base from which to pull back.* An enforced compliance strategy keeps the opposition extremely busy contesting and adjusting to regulations; it allows for limited accommodation at a later date. Having established its ground, the OSM pulled back, in regard to negotiations on state primacy, to field-level discretion, and to regulations (e.g., sedimentation ponds and the state window). It remains to be seen, but it is likely, that the base of stringent rules will have a long-term constraining effect on the Reagan administration's turn toward negotiated compliance strategies.

(5) An enforced compliance strategy *provides an agency with an external base of support.* All regulatory agencies are faced with conflicting demands. By *not* attempting to make everyone happy, the agency at least enlists solid support from one party. For the Office of Surface Mining, the enforced compliance model solidified the support of environmentalist organizations. The EPA, which chose a more moderate course, received less vigorous environmentalist support (Marcus, 1980).

(6) An enforced compliance strategy *provides an agency with a strong sense of mission.* In contrast, a negotiated compliance strategy may leave the agency's mission in doubt. For the participants, the construction of a new agency is not just another day at the office; it demands a nonbureaucratic workday. In the case of the OSM, a negotiated compliance strategy would have appeared contradictory to the perceived legislative mandate. The development of a sense of special purpose provided early OSM employees with the motivational ground for meeting heavy demands. The originators of the regulatory program felt that they were involved in a significant and exciting task; they still look back to that period with nostalgia. Strong enforced compliance strategies were important sources for

establishing a sense of mission in other new-style agencies as well (Kelman, 1980; Marcus, 1980).

(7) An enforced compliance strategy may be *a source of internal cohesion within a new agency*. A sense of unity is extremely important as a counter to the many controversies and debates produced by program-building. The internalization of a sense of mission is a source of organizational solidarity. By restricting negotiations with those to be regulated, the Office of Surface Mining engendered a spirit of unification against known adversaries. This sense of cohesion developed both at headquarters and in the regions, but to a more limited extent between the two.

(8) A strategy of enforced compliance *allows a new agency to avoid a strict hierarchical pattern of control*. Theories of mechanistic organization would lead one to expect that a rigidly legalistic program would be carried out by means of centralized authoritarian control (Burns and Stalker, 1961). But, for the OSM (at least initially), common values and a mandate for legalistic application of stringent rules allowed for bureaucratic decentralization. The rules themselves specified what needed to be done. With one expection—Region West—the regions felt themselves bound by the rules. Thus, the Office of Surface Mining was able to operate effectively through relatively autonomous regional offices.

## Costs of Enforced Compliance

(1) An enforced compliance strategy *neglects the practical politics of implementation*. Although the enforced compliance tactic is itself a political strategy, it is a strategy that assumes strong political and power bases and eschews coalitions. An agency that sharply limits the negotiation of compliance must operate on the basis of a strong mandate. The Office of Surface Mining assumed that it had such a mandate. Therefore, it felt that it could fairly easily withstand the political pressures of the coal industry. It would simply force the industry to comply with the act of Congress. Although agency officials denied that they ever intended to take an adversarial position toward the states, they did acknowledge taking the states for granted. When a number of the states revolted against the agency's high-handness, the OSM suddenly found that it had nearly lost its congressional support.

There were at least two reasons for the agency's lack of political savvy. First, there was the constraint of time. The agency was under such heavy pressure to promulgate and implement the regulations that it was oblivious to the need for fine-tuned negotiations with the states and for maintaining open lines of communication with Congress. Second, whatever the beliefs of agency officials, the logic of their enforced compliance strategy placed them in an adversarial position in relation to the states. The agency, after all, was demanding a minimally negotiated form of compliance from the states as well as from the coal industry. At the time of the states' revolt, Congress was willing to accept a negotiated compliance policy for the state, even though it desired an enforced compliance strategy toward the coal industry.

(2) An enforced compliance strategy *maximizes opposition to an agency.* The long struggle to enact the SMCRA had sharply polarized the issue. The tough stance taken by the agency led the coal industry to believe that many of the battles they had won in the making of the law were now being lost in the making of the regulations and in the strict conditions for primacy. The industry was being challenged to fight back, and it did. More importantly, the states followed suit.

(3) An enforced compliance strategy *escalates the level of hostility.* At all stages and levels of the regulatory process, the OSM presented a single message, "Be reasonable, do it *our* way." The OSM managed to (a) threaten the autonomy of state governors by usurping states' "rights" (e.g., by demanding that the states revise statutes other than their mining laws); (b) question the professional integrity of state regulatory officials (e.g., by ignoring their claims of special knowledge of local conditions); (c) irritate the major coal industry officials (e.g., by keeping them at a distance from agency decision making); and (d) enrage local coal operators (e.g., by enforcing against minor violations, demanding payment of fines before a hearing, maintaining many fines even though a violation had been abated in the appropriate time, by ignoring site-specific mining and reclamation practices). The OSM's policies drove a few state governors and a multitude of coal operators into a frenzy of vituperation. There is marked similarity between the OSM and the OSHA in their enforcement policies and in the immediately damaging and hostile responses evoked by these policies (cf. Kelman, 1980).

(4) An enforced compliance strategy *unites the opposition* to a regulatory agency. A primary component of a strict legalistic policy is equal treatment of those to be controlled. Lack of a discretionary policy means that no group receives special treatment because of distinctive problems or because of lack of problems. The Office of Surface Mining had a clear tendency to produce and implement regulations on the basis of a "worst case" mentality. That is, the agency often wrote rules in order to prevent the worst known cases of environmental degradation from recurring. The rule then was applied to all operators, despite the diversity within the industry. Individual coal operators have little in common. Thus, some faced major difficulties in compliance, others few. Some were more willing to comply than others. This same worst case orientation was evident in the agency's relations with the states. The states vary in environmental problems and in internal pressures to accommodate the coal industry. Through its egalitarian, universalistic policies the OSM unified its opponents—big and small coal, East and West, states with good programs and those with poor ones. Those who felt abused because they were forced to revise environmentally sound mining practices were driven into the same camp with those who felt abused by the imposition of any controls whatsoever. Certainly, in pursuing a policy of enforced compliance, the agency ignored the ancient wisdom of "divide and conquer."

(5) An enforced compliance policy *maximizes litigation.* If conflict between two parties is not managed by negotiation, there are few options available for its resolution other than the courts. The OSM assumed, probably correctly, that the coal industry would test the program in court, no matter what it did. Through a spiral of mutual anticipation of the worst, this prophecy became self-fulfilling.

(6) An enforced compliance strategy tends to *maximize the cost of compliance.* By enforcing compliance with design criteria and standards, without regard for special individual circulstances or for situations where the mine operator could meet performance standards by alternative means, the agency increased production costs by a greater amount than would be required through a negotiated compliance strategy. There is no sure way of determining exactly this incremental cost, which provided the coal industry with a handy tool for beating on the regulatory agency. In any event, increased operator costs may decrease the social costs of

production. The arguments favoring enforced compliance through design standards are as follows: (1) environmental damage will be more limited than if failure-prone techniques for meeting performance standards are used, and (2) inspections for design standards limit the costs of enforcement. There is an interesting irony here. The new social regulation is largely an attempt to control the social costs (i.e., the externalities) of production. Design standards are mechanisms by which the regulatory agency externalizes *its* costs back upon the externalizers. Put another way, design standards represent a strategy for the double internalization of social costs— the social costs of production and the social costs of control.

(7) *In the long run,* an enforced compliance style *generates internal conflict* in an agency. Legalistic rules and stringent enforcement generally are favored by lawyers and central administrators. Implementation is carried out in the field by technical experts. Such experts generally wish to use discretion and negotiated compliance in their work. They turn in this direction out of professional pride in their specialized knowledge and abilities, out of recognition of viable alternatives in obtaining compliance, and often out of a sense of identification with the regulated. Generally the OSM's regional directors went by the book, but fought with headquarters for more realistic, technically feasible revisions of the regulations. The majority of inspectors in all regions desired greater discretion in their enforcement activities. A central paradox of the enforced compliance model is that it is a system based on legal and technical expertise that tends to breakdown because it ignores its own specialists.

## POLICY IMPLICATIONS

An easy conclusion that might be drawn from the preceding discussion is that an extreme enforced compliance strategy is likely to generate costs that threaten to erode its benefits. Next we examine variations on that theme in the form of tentative policy statements derived from our analysis. We state these as correctives for an agency that has a mandate for strict enforcement policies. Our comments take the form of a conservative critique of the OSM's program—conservative in the sense that we fundamentally accept the position that the program, as initially constructed, was basically a sound and effective means of implementing the act.

Most of the deficiencies we discuss were brought to our attention by respondents who were agency executives and managers during the Carter administration. Major deficiencies in the OSM's policy implementation include the following: (a) failures of communication with the states, Congress, the regions, and with industry; (b) insufficient flexibility in many of the regulations (generally in over-reliance on design standards— particularly in areas such as sedimentation ponds, permit analysis, seeding, bonding, and the point system for assessment of fines); (c) lack of attention to the difficulties of the small operators; (d) overcentralized and rigid assessment procedures; (e) inability to collect fines; and (f) insufficient discretion in the hands of the regions and the individual inspectors. We now turn to some broader policy implications that can be assessed from the deficiencies in OSM's operational style.

(1) In the short run, mandated early deadlines are important in establishing agency autonomy and in ensuring that an agency's mandate for action will not be sidetracked. The legislation of mandatory timetables for regulatory agencies was initiated in a number of environmental protection laws in the early 1970s and was intended to prevent the capture of the EPA by regulated industries (Marcus, 1980). It was generally recognized that the ineffectiveness of earlier environmental laws could be traced in part to the lack of precise deadlines. The SMCRA went beyond previous environmental protection statutes in specifying deadlines for detailed rules as well as for meeting specific goals. The further specification of timetables was based, no doubt, on knowledge of rule-making delays in both the EPA and OSHA (cf. Kelman, 1980). Although the deadlines imposed on the EPA caused many problems, two separate studies conclude that they were partially effective (National Research Council, 1977; marcus, 1980). Ackerman and Hassler (1981) refer to congressional attempts to direct the actions of the new social regulatory agencies as "agenda-forcing" statutes. Clearly time-forcing statutory deadlines are an aspect of agenda-forcing. What were the consequences of statutory time-forcing for the Office of Surface Mining?

Time constraints on the production of the regulations prevented the full consideration of all technical options. Flexible technical alternatives were often rejected for legal reasons; there was no time for reformulation of these suggestions. In general, the pressing deadlines placed decisive power in the hands of the attorneys who wrote the final draft. Interested parties had little time to respond adequately to the proposed regulations—a particularly difficult constraint for small industry. Then, in the review of these comments, the agency had insufficient time to review any but those that were fully justified, technically and legally. Less stringent deadlines would have allowed for more detailed, face-to-face negotiation on particular details. More flexible regulations, less litigation, and less polarization of attitudes might have resulted. Because the agency was forced to give priority to getting the job done on time, it isolated itself and gave insufficient attention to the problem of communication with the states, with Congress, and with the coal industry. Thus, time constraints led agency officials to neglect the political context of their activities.

(2) The construction of an effective regulatory program must be based on a recognition of political forces. To rephrase Clausowitz' aphorism on war, "The regulatory process is the continuation of political struggle by other means." Regulators would like to place themselves above and beyond politics, to believe that their task is simply the application of administrative, legal, and technical expertise. Both the EPA and the OSHA tried to isolate themselves from White House pressure in order to maintain their autonomy and relatively stringent regulatory postures (Marcus, 1980; Kelman, 1980). In at least one instance, the OSM also fought against interference from the executive branch. In general, however, the weakness of the OSM political liaison was due to neglect rather than intention. Although the Office of Surface Mining was a creature of Congress and subject to its oversight, the agency paid little attention to keeping the lines of communication open. Even before the OSM was established, both the OSHA and the EPA had been subjected to congressional attack because of their stringent enforcement policies. The OSM's failure to keep Congress informed resulted in greater opposition to a rigorous program than might have been the case otherwise. This opposition eased the way for the agency's radical change in direction under the Reagan administration.

Although some of the states would have fought the OSM under any circumstances, the support of others could have been obtained through direct contact with irate governors and an earlier extension of the primary deadline. By securing the support of a few key states, the agency could have prevented the unification of the opposition. When states with strong programs opposed the agency's policies, it justified the opposition of states with weak programs, which in turn justified the opposition of the coal industry. By neglecting any political base other than the environmentalist community, the Office of Surface Mining permitted its opposition to snowball. A major source of the agency's problems was its failure to realize that it was involved in a game of coalitional politics.

(3) Accommodative negotiation must be a strategic component of even the strongest enforced compliance regulatory program. Negotiation is a built-in aspect of any regulatory process. In the case of the OSM, negotiation was required, for example, in the rule-making process and in the review of state programs. But in nearly every instance, these negotiations had a formal, legalistic, adversarial character. Although not mandated by statute, both the OSHA and the EPA often include face-to-face discussions with both state and industry at an early point in the rule-making process (National Research Council, 1977). Many state surface mining regulatory agencies also use this procedure. A number of OSM officials, especially those in the field, would have preferred such direct negotiations. It is likely that such meetings would have aided the production of more workable regulations, at the cost, however, of some delay. It must be recognized that the enabling statute placed some serious limitations on negotiation. For example, the requirement for "best available technology" in preventing siltation limited the possibility of using more appropriate technologies to meet the statutory goals.

The agency's most striking failure to engage in accommodative negotiations was in its relations with the states. In the rule-making process, the states were treated much the same way as industry. Negotiations were basically limited to public hearings and to the formal submission of complaints and alternatives, to which the agency formally replied through the *Federal Register*. Dialogue was not an important part of the process. A symbolic component of the relationship was the *ex parte* solicitor's opinion, which cut off any communications with the states after the end of the public comment period. In the words of a solicitor, this opinion "was legally correct, but a political disaster." Initially, the states were treated in the same adversarial manner in the primacy process. The agency's lack of accommodation was motivated by a desire to ensure tough state programs. If more states had obtained approved programs and had been satisfied with them before the change in presidential administrations, it is likely that they would have opposed a massive rewriting of the regulations. In the long run, the tough stance toward the states may have weakened their programs. The lesson to be learned here is that in trying to win every battle, you may lose the war.

(4) Flexible regulations are not necessarily bad regulations. Major complaints against the OSM's regulations included the failure to allow for variations in local conditions and the overreliance on design standards. By the end of their tenure, most OSM executives from the Carter administration were coming to see the validity of some of these criticisms. As previously noted, the lack of flexibility in the regulations reflected a worst case orientation toward the law. As a task force member and headquarters executive told us:

> We tended to write regulations, I think, . . . for the worst case.
> . . . [T]here was kind of a stated joke in the agency—not a joke,
> I mean, but it tells the story: "Well, if we write the regulation this
> way, can we make Virginia do it?" Virginia being, probably, the
> worst state in the country for regulating.

To paraphrase a comment quoted earlier, "Rigid regulations were environmentally sound, but they were a political disaster."
In the long run, it seems inescapable that political support for rigid regulations could not have been maintained, even had there been no turnover in administrations. All parties agreed that compliance with the law on the basis of flexible regulations was possible. The real question was the *probability* of compliance, a question of trust. It is possible that the protest against inflexible rules may result in weaker rules than would have ensued if the rules had been more flexible in the first place. As indicated in the National Research Council report on surface mining (1981b), design standards can be modified to meet local conditions in ways that are environmentally and legally sound.
Finally, it is interesting to note that Kelman (1981) found that the regulations for protecting occupational safety and health are more flexible in social democratic Sweden than in the United States. This greater flexibility is possible because of the context of a greater spirit of trust between industry and state regulators than is found in the United States. Paradoxically, the inflexibility of the OSM's rules reflected the U.S. coal industry's great potential power to subvert the regulatory process.

(5) Discretion is a necessary and unavoidable component of an effective implementation program. The OSM made a bow to discretionary enforcement policies in its organizational structure by permitting some regional autonomy. Nevertheless, the regions were guided by and were expected to implement the strategy of strict enforced compliance emanating from headquarters. But no guidelines were ever established for resolving the contradictory demands of regional variations and national uniformity. Only the Region West was able to develop a distinctive approach to enforcement. Regulation there through the process of permit review rather than by stringent I & E procedures—appropriate in Region West because of the presence of federal coal and because of the long lead time needed to plan large mines—gradually was accepted as a viable enforcement alternative. A similar regulatory policy would be to license coal operators and regulate by means of revocation or denial of such licenses. Unfortunately, this strategy, employed in Pennsylvania, was not provided in the SMCRA.

The regional directors chafed against the strictures of rigorous enforced compliance policies, and they sought more discretion and clearer guidelines for their use. Had the Washington office paid more attention to the regional directors, the regulations would have been more flexible and the implementation procedures more discretionary. It is likely that the implementation program would have aroused less hostility and been more effective if the assessment and collection of fines had been conducted at the regional level, if discretionary elimination of fines through abatement of the violation had been allowed, and if inspectors had been given more discretion in writing citations. Office of Surface Mining inspectors, like their counterparts in a number of other agencies (Hawkins, 1980; Kagan, 1980), believed that they could have gained compliance from operators more effectively if they had been allowed more discretion.

## CONCLUSIONS

On the basis of its statutory mandate, its value-laden choices, and its external constraints, the early Office of Surface Mining quickly developed a regulatory style oriented toward gaining compliance through stringent enforcement rather than accommodative negotiation. Generally, this enforcing style was effective. The agency rapidly produced tough, detailed rules for limiting environmental damage from surface mining. It enforced

these rules uniformly and vigorously. It demanded exacting state programs. There can be little doubt that the environment was improved
by these actions. Many coal operators were forced to improve their
mining practices and many states were pushed to strengthen their surface
mining laws, regulations, and enforcement practices. The immediate
beneficiaries of the OSM's actions were the residents of the coal fields.
Generally grass root citizens' groups were pleased with the OSM's
policies and performance.

The regulatory program was costly for the coal industry, especially
for small Appalachian operators. However, firms passed on part of the
costs of regulated coal production to consumers. A more costly burden
of regulation for the coal operators was the loss of autonomy in planning,
mining, and reclamation practices. Similarly, state regulators paid the
price of diminished independence.

The focus of our discussion of the costs of enforced compliance policies
has been on the internal costs borne by the OSM itself. The burden of
our argument is that an extreme enforced compliance style feeds back
upon itself to its own detriment. Since the regulatory process is not
conducted in a vacuum, some allowance for flexibility and negotiation
is a tactical necessity for the implementation of a long-range enforced
compliance strategy. The Office of Surface Mining's basic strategy was
an overreaction to the theory of incremental agency capture. In turn,
it helped stimulate a counter-reaction. Nevertheless, our emphasis on
the internal costs of a strong regulatory style should not be overdrawn.
Since the reaction against the OSM's early program was overdetermined
by external forces, no amount of ducking and weaving could have
forestalled the radical reversal in the direction taken by the agency
under the Reagan administration.

In *The Politics of Regulation,* James Q. Wilson (1980) argues that
regulatory agencies can be categorized in terms of the external distribution of costs and benefits. When the proposed costs are narrowly
concentrated and the expected benefits are widely distributed, regulation
can only emerge from "entrepreneurial politics." Like other new social
regulatory agencies, the Office of Surface Mining originated when skilled
entrepreneurs were able to mobilize resources and generate widespread
public support for surface mining legislation. The direct costs were to
be borne by a particular industry; the direct benefits would accrue to
a very small interest group—coal field residents. But the indirect benefits
deriving from the prevention of environmental degradation would be
widespread.

Entrepreneurs may fade and public interest may wane. The future of
surface mining regulation hangs on the ability of environmentalist en-

trepreneurs to marshal resources for litigation and renewed political struggle. The prospect certainly is not dim. If the old-style regulatory agencies were subject to a life cycle tending toward senesence and capture (Bernstein, 1955), it is likely that the new-style agencies, such as the Office of Surface Mining, will be rejuvenated in periods of politically charged reform. Given large industry's need for stability and predictability, the ability to maintain a state of regulatory uncertainty may be the best weapon available to reformers.

# CODA
# The Office of Surface Mining Since 1980

In his election campaign, Ronald Reagan sounded three themes that later found expression in his appointees and in the regulatory policies they enunciated. He expressed a determined faith in the "free enterprise system" and its ability, if unfettered, to provide economic prosperity for the American people and growth for the American economy. At the same time, he railed against overregulation as an economically harmful process that impeded American productivity. It was time, he charged, to throw off the yoke of government regulation so that business once again could exercise its creativity, provide jobs for American workers, and increase productivity. Finally, Reagan charged that the federal government had usurped too many powers and prerogatives that properly belong to the states.

Reagan pledged that, if elected, he would launch a program of "regulatory reform" to remove regulations and regulatory apparatuses that were burdensome, cost-effective, and counter-productive for American business. Coupled with this pledge was a promise to enhance the power and responsibility of state governments. Following his election, President Reagan moved to implement these political commitments.

During the transition to the new administration, the conservative Heritage Foundation subjected the Office of Surface Mining to critical scrutiny (Heatherly, 1981). The report scorned the OSM for its "zealotry" in promulgating regulations "far in excess" of the requirements of the act and charged it with having completely excluded "developmental interests" (Heatherly, 1981:345). The report recommended that the new president and secretary of the interior "make an example of OSM and its regulatory excesses and . . . place high priority on an early transition to a State lead concept." Changes in both the act and OSM's regulations were urged. Additionally, the new administration was urged to return power to the states, to reduce the OSM's enforcement staff, to cut the agency's budget, and to replace "current OSM senior staff and regional directors with professionals more attuned to a rational program" of reclamation (Heatherly, 1981:346–47).

## THE NEW OSM LEADERSHIP

President Reagan's new secretary of the interior was James Watt, a westerner who had strong developmental biases. Prior to his selection as secretary, Watt helped found and worked as an attorney for the Mountain States Legal Foundation, a conservative "public-interest" law firm that had opposed the OSM and environmentalist groups in appellate litigation. The new secretary was a strident, outspoken critic of environmentalists and of governmental policies that reflected their views. Moreover, he openly expressed sympathy for the "Sagebrush Rebellion," a western-based movement of state and local officials and landowners who attacked what they saw as an intrusive, heavy-handed federal presence in "their" region of the United States.

Watt's appointment touched off a storm of protest from the eastern media and environmentalist and citizens' groups around the country. Editorial critics charged that he was biased toward developmentalism, at the expense of even the most moderate environmental reforms.

Almost within hours of Reagan's inauguration, Watt held a mass meeting with Department of Interior employees. Uncompromisingly, he informed them that "the American people" had given a mandate for change; those who felt they could not work for change were invited to search for employment. As is customary, OSM's political appointees— among them the agency director—resigned and the Secretary appointed a career civil servant as acting director. Several months elapsed before the top leadership positions in the agency were filled. During the interim period, environmentalists charged that the day-to-day operation of the OSM was conducted by personnel in the Department of Interior who had helped write the Heritage Foundation critique of it.

Watt appointed to top OSM positions two individuals from states that had most vigorously resisted the agency's efforts. Among OSM personnel and environmentalists, these appointments created concern about the agency's potential for even-handedness. In Senate hearings, the OSM director-designate made it clear that he shared the new administration's view of the "new federalism." The new managers of the OSM established a new agenda with two major components: reorganization and regulatory reform.

## OSM REORGANIZATION

Relations between new appointees and older employees often were strained during the early months of the new administration. The agency contained two distinct alignments of personnel: those who criticized and those who supported planned reorganization. The morale of old-line personnel suffered greatly. Many feared that surface mining regulation would revert to pre-1978 conditions.

Monthly Washington meetings between headquarters executives and regional staff were discontinued. Regional directors were left in a state of uncertainty, while the newly-appointed headquarters executives made decisions about the agency's future. In May of 1981, the regional directors were informed that the entire agency would be reorganized.

The reorganization plan replaced regional offices with fourteen state offices, supported by six field offices and two technical service centers. State offices were located in the major coal-producing states. An eastern technical service center was located in Pittsburgh; a comparable western center was to be located in Casper, Wyoming (later shifted, under congressional pressure, to Denver). Headquarters also was reorganized to reduce the five original assistant director positions to three. Overall, the number of OSM personnel was reduced sharply, with major cuts occurring in the inspection and enforcement.program.

## REGULATORY REFORM

The other half of the new agenda for the OSM was regulatory reform. The OSM's new leadership developed a *Schedule for Regulatory Reform* (OSM, 1981) to accomplish six objectives:

(1.) Removal of excessive federal regulations
(2.) Return of surface coal mining regulation to the states

(3.) Development of more cost-effective regulation
(4.) Assurance of continuity in state programs in order to maintain coal productivity
(5.) Minimum regulatory authority involvement in the development and design of mining operations
(6.) Technical guidance and leadership to the states


Department of Interior leadership opted for a regulatory reform approach designed to support state primacy goals. Agency resources were refocused on working with the states to develop acceptable state programs. One of the first steps in this process was a move to delete the state window provision of the permanent program regulations.[1] By doing so, the new Interior and OSM leadership intended to give the states greater latitude to tailor their regulatory programs to local problems and conditions. The revised state window regulation explicitly replaced the requirement that state regulations be "no less stringent than" the federal regulations with the requirement that they be "no less effective than" the latter. Predictably, environmentalists charged that this change amounted to boarding up the state window. This revision served as an important symbolic signal to the states that the new administration intended to change regulatory directions and to assist them to acquire primacy.

After 1981 the OSM engaged in an extensive revision of numerous portions of the permanent program. Originally it was thought that the rewrite project could be accomplished quickly but numerous delays developed out of an operational contradiction between the new leadership's twin objectives of reorganization and regulatory reform. In the process of reducing the number of agency employees and relocating offices, the OSM lost many of the technical personnel it needed to revise regulations. Also, the new leadership encountered legal obstacles to rapid, wholesale changes in regulations when environmentalist and public-interest groups initiated litigation.

## INSPECTION AND ENFORCEMENT

The new OSM leadership generally adopted a negotiated compliance approach to inspection and enforcement. The agency's new executives and Interior officials made it unmistakably clear that they wanted a diminished federal regulatory effort. For example, OSM's acting director instituted a new policy on the handling and distribution of cessation orders. Field inspectors were now required to secure Washington approval before issuing a CO to a mining firm. Moreover, field solicitors were informed that future cases of OSM-initiated litigation would require prior approval from the Washington Solicitor's Office. The new OSM leadership moved one more step to dampen the stringency of the inspection and enforcement program by initiating a revision of the relevant permanent program regulations.

These policy changes were unmistakable signals that, henceforth, the preferred regulatory style at the OSM would *not* be enforced compliance.

## STATE RESPONSES

True to its promises, the new agency leadership worked with the states in the process of regulatory reform and the push for primacy. Regulatory revision reflected many state concerns. Still, there were strains and problems in the OSM relationship with the states. Some states simply resisted efforts by the new OSM personnel to establish and implement even a minimally effective regulatory program. Others continued to engage in collusive actions with coal operators to evade the spirit, if not the intent of the Surface Mining Act and the interim program regulations. In short, the new OSM executives learned that some states are unyielding in their one-sided demand for regulatory flexibility.

State reactions to the new OSM and its regulatory programs varied substantially during its first years. On one hand, states west of the Mississippi River worked diligently with the agency to develop satisfactory regulatory programs and to acquire primacy. On the other hand, midwestern and Appalachian states delayed the movement toward primacy. Seven states, all east of the Mississippi River, took advantage of section 503(d) of the act to stall the move toward primacy. In each of these states, state court judges issued injunctions that prohibited the submission to OSM of state primacy applications. Hopeful that the new OSM leadership would be less demanding, some eastern states resubmitted weakened programs rejected earlier by OSM.

## THE COAL INDUSTRY

Despite their obvious unity in wanting little or no federal controls, large and small coal producers face very different economic constraints. Large producers have in-house technical and legal staffs that prepare permit applications, but most small producers must hire outside consultants for these tasks. For the small, economically-marginal producer, large increases in permitting costs threaten continued operation. Blasting regulations are less bothersome to large producers that employ trained blasters and are relocated in unpopulated areas where restrictive blasting regulations do not apply. Therefore, inspection and enforcement actions never were symbolic irritants for large producers to the same degree that they were for small producers. Given these differences in their operations and concerns, it is not surprising that fissures appeared in the coalition of large and small coal producers.

Small, economically-marginal coal producers wanted to destroy the OSM so that never again would it threaten them and their operations. Since the combination of higher permitting, bonding and reclamation costs, and a slumping coal market had pushed many of them to the point of insolvency, they demanded sweeping changes in the federal regulations. Just as they supported organizational emasculation of the OSM, they also advocated changes in the regulatory standards the states must meet to acquire primacy. They hoped that, once the regulatory task was returned to the states, small coal producers once again would flourish.

Understandably they pressed for severe reductions in regulatory requirements and easier access to public monies provided by the Small Operators' Assistance Program. First, they pushed for a redefinition of "small operator" so that companies that mine a larger volume of coal would be eligible for assistance. Second, they advocated an increase in the type of assistance given to small operators under the program.

When it became apparent to large coal producers that increased oversight was unavoidable, their objectives shifted from defeat of regulatory legislation to construction of an enforcement program consistent with their economic interests. To maximize their operating flexibility, they pushed to achieve a program emphasizing performance (rather than design) standards. Because they employed trained experts, large producers could adjust to a legalistic and highly technocratic regulatory process. In contrast to small operators, they did not oppose requirements that reclamation structures and processes be designed by "registered" professionals. Large coal was more willing to live with the regulations so long as the means of reaching regulatory goals could be determined by their own technical experts.

Coupled with large coal's desire for flexibility in regulatory requirements is the need for certainty and predictability. Because of their size and capital needs, large coal must be able to plan years ahead if they are to attract capital and estimate profits. Certainly they welcomed the new OSM leadership and were hopeful of major modifications of the federal and state programs; however, they feared that radical changes would create a backlash and, thus, wholesale revisions in regulatory policy under a future administration. Large coal wanted to avoid radical swings in policy.

## ENVIRONMENTAL AND CITIZENS' GROUPS

Under the Carter administration, citizens' and environmentalist groups could count on receiving sympathetic hearings at various levels of the Department of the Interior. After the change in presidential administrations, there was a 180 degree shift in relations between citizens' groups and the OSM. Relations between the agency and the environmentalist community have grown adversarial. Environmentalists generally believe that the new administration has tried to decimate the agency so that it is totally incapable of maintaining a credible regulatory posture. The most optimistic among them believes that these efforts cannot succeed because the act itself is so stringent; the more pessimistic almost despair at the consequences of returning responsibility for regulation to the states. To retard the pace of regulatory reform, environmental organizations filed numerous suits against the OSM, charging it with procedural errors in its efforts to rewrite the permanent program regulations.

## CONCLUSIONS

The 1980 election of President Reagan produced immediate, massive changes in the state's role in social regulation. Reagan interpreted his election as a popular mandate for regulatory reform—that is, a sharp reduction of federal control of business activities, including production practices related to health, safety, and the environment.[2] The Office of Surface Mining was one of the first agencies to undergo reorganization and procedural changes at the hands of the Reagan administration.

An array of theories specify factors that contribute to the capture of state agencies by the regulated parties (Mitnick, 1980). These factors include vague statutes, monopolization of technical knowledge by the regulated industry, interchange of personnel, and declining support from reform groups. None of the theories is as simple as what actually happened—a democratic coup d'etat or *capture from above.* Reagan's top replacements in the OSM were opposed ideologically to previous policies. Three key replacements were people who had been vigorous opponents of its policies. Taking office while the agency was making the transition from federal to state primacy in enforcement, the new state managers of OSM immediately reorganized its administrative structure (giving *more* power to the central office), sharply reduced its work-force, modified its enforcement standards, and began a major revision of the regulations. As was the case at the EPA, the OSM experienced a massive crisis of morale. Here we have an example of the relevance of strong form special interest theory—instrumentalist control of an agency by a regulated fraction of capital.[3]

But can such capture really be complete? Does law on the books—statutes, regulations, previous court decisions—mean nothing at all? The Reagan administration did not view the statute as a major problem. It chose to rewrite the regulations rather than attempt to change the law. Even though the regulations were directly controlled by appointed state managers, the OSM replacement confronted five constraints: (1) statutory provisions were often quite specific; (2) the majority of OSM workers were holdovers, committed to the old regulations; (3) large coal wished to avoid massive regulation changes that would provoke a reaction in a later administration;(4) environmentalists were willing to take court action; and (5) many of the regulations had been sustained in previous court decisions. For these reasons, it took the Reagan administration more than two years to rewrite the regulations. After three rounds of lawsuits, it lost on most major issues. Thus, in disputes between state managers, the hammer belongs to the judge. These developments seem to provide strong support for the concept of the "relative autonomy of the law," in this case, administrative law. Administrative law incorporates the outcome of previous class struggle and state managerial autonomy. The relative autonomy of law prevents full capture of the state.

Finally, what has been the new administration's record on oversight of state programs and enforcement? OSM has intentionally adopted a negotiated compliance style of regulation (weak in the eyes of reformers), evidenced by extended deadlines to state programs, fewer inspections than required by law, and limited citations. Nevertheless, the new OSM managers have continued the old fights with a number of local state program managers. For example, the OSM has found it necessary to revoke authority for inspection and enforcement in Oklahoma and Tennessee (small coal producers) and has threatened a takeover in Kentucky (a major producer). Thus, it appears that federal state managers, even those with direct ties to coal producers, find themselves constrained by law and by position to adopt an unexpected and unwanted autonomy from the coal industry and the local state managers who are constrained to act in the interests of local capital.

# Appendix
# Methodology

As conceived originally, our primary research objective was to develop a detailed understanding and theoretical interpretation of the forces, both from within and without, that shape a new regulatory agency and program. We planned to make extensive use of participant observation as a data collection technique and to focus both on agency policy making and its field-level implementation in two distinctively different coal-producing regions of the United States.

We approached headquarters executives of the Office of Surface Mining—rather naively as it turned out—with our proposal and asked for their cooperation. They expressed an interest in the project's objectives and readily provided assurances that the research could proceed. However, nearly a year elapsed between this initial contact with headquarters and the start of data collection. During this interim period, the agency came under intense attack on a variety of fronts, and its regional office personnel faced severe work pressures mandated by the agency's enabling statute. Consequently, when we moved to begin data collection in two of the agency's five regional offices, managers in the designated offices balked. Data collection was stalled for several months while we renegotiated the terms of the research agreement. Eventually we secured regional cooperation, but only on the condition that our plans for participant observation be dropped.

We employed five methodological techniques in the course of the research: (1) archival analysis, (2) personal interviews, (3) a mail questionnaire, (4) analysis of personal documents, and (5) analysis of secondary reports and analyses of the Office of Surface Mining and its operations. Here we give a brief overview of our methods; specific data collection techniques are detailed at appropriate places in the remainder of the report.

We examined trade publications of the coal industry spanning a period of nearly fifteen years, concentrating on the interval between 1968 and passage of the act in 1977. The most useful publications here were the *Mining Congress Journal* and *Coal Age,* though we also examined some issues of trade publications representing the viewpoints of smaller coal producers (e.g., the *National Independent Coal Leader*). We scrutinized published hearings held by congressional committees and subcommittees during the period when Congress was considering federal legislation to regulate surface coal mining (1968–1977). Also, we examined all subsequent House and Senate committee reports on oversight of the OSM.

We collected and examined numerous OSM internal reports and memoranda on the emerging regulatory program, its reception and impact, and the agency's relations with its various constituencies. We secured and analyzed routine, periodic statistical reports on the agency's inspection and enforcement operations. Additionally, we selected a sample of eighty-three coal mining firms and examined OSM's inspection and enforcement records for all enforcement actions taken against the companies during an eighteen-month period in 1978–1980. Data from the files were coded and analyzed to determine the major variables that affect enforcement activities, especially the magnitude of civil fines assessed for violations of the agency's regulations.

Members of the research team attended eight public hearings—all in southern Appalachia—held by the OSM to collect public comments on portions of its emerging regulatory programs. We examined the transcripts of numerous other hearings of the same type for regions outside southern Appalachia.

In addition to these archival data, personal interviews were conducted with 154 persons. Many of the respondents were interviewed two or more times so that we conducted approximately 180 interviews. Overwhelmingly, the majority of the interviews were conducted in Washington, D.C., and the two OSM regions targeted in our proposal. Although most of the interviews were face-to-face, approximately ten were conducted by telephone. The majority of the interviews were tape-recorded and later transcribed for analysis. However, physical circumstances and the preferences of respondents did not always permit us to record the interviews. In such situations, we relied on field notes made either during the interview or immediately following its conclusion.

OSM respondents ranged from field-level personnel to the highest ranking executives at the headquarters level. We also interviewed personnel in the Department of the Interior, including the Solicitor's Office, whose attorneys represent the Office of Surface Mining. Exclusive of the agency itself, the personal interviews included congressional staff members and former staff members, former White House personnel, representatives of environmentalist and other citizens' groups, representatives of coal industry, trade and lobbying organizations, employees and officers of numerous mining companies, and personnel in a number of state-level surface mining regulatory agencies. Table A-1 summarizes the numbers and types of individuals who were interviewed.

As Table A-1 indicates, we interviewed forty-three OSM inspectors and former inspectors regarding the regulatory process at the field level. However, because the inspection and enforcement program was a special research focus, we constructed a mail questionnaire that was used to collect comparable data for OSM's entire inspector corps. The questionnaire, which is discussed in greater detail in chapter 7, was mailed in July, 1981, to all remaining OSM inspectors (N = 158). Replies were received from 126 inspectors (79.8 percent).

TABLE A-1
SUMMARY DESCRIPTION OF INTERVIEW RESPONDENTS

| Type of Respondent/Group | Number |
|---|---|
| OSM Personnel | |
| Headquarters Personnel: | |
| Executives | 9 |
| Others (e.g., branch chiefs) | 3 |
| Regional Level: | |
| Managers | 11 |
| Others (e.g., field supervisors, inspectors) | 43 |
| Interior Department | |
| Executives | 2 |
| Solicitors | 6 |
| Coal Industry | |
| Mining Companies | 38 |
| Trade Associations/Lobbying Organizations | 9 |
| Mining Consultants & Related Industry (e.g., heavy equipment salespersons) | 6 |
| Environmentalist Organizations | |
| National | 4 |
| Regional | 6 |
| State Personnel | |
| Managers | 6 |
| Others (e.g., field supervisors, inspectors) | 8 |
| Others (e.g. congressional staff, White House aides) | 3 |
| TOTAL | 154 |

A number of OSM personnel or former personnel shared with us personal materials they compiled or collected during their tenure in the agency. Also, several individuals virtually opened their files to us, enabling us to examine a variety of materials, such as internal memoranda and policy option papers that would not have been available otherwise.

Finally, we examined available published research on the surface coal mining process and the Office of Surface Mining (e.g., National Research Council, 1980, 1981; Menzel et al., 1980; Weiner, 1980). Several coal companies and industry trade associations gave us copies of their own studies on the impact of the OSM's regulatory program. Likewise, environmentalist groups helped us greatly by providing copies of some of their studies of surface mining regulation (e.g., Save our Cumberland Mountains, n.d.; Environmental Policy Center, 1982).

# Notes

## 1 Regulation and the State

1. The process of surface mining and the strictures of the federal law are described more fully in chapters 2 and 3.

2. Corporations are created through law and are subjected increasingly to legal restrictions. Corporate crimes and legal offenses are defined by state actions—criminal law, certainly, but more importantly regulatory law. In general, the targets of regulatory law and agencies are "legal persons" (corporations). Real people commit "crimes"; legal persons commit "offenses." In our example, the surface mining corporation that leaves a highwall has committed a regulatory violation or offense; however, few people regard such violations as criminal acts. Although officials of the offending company could be subjected to criminal sanctions, such an eventuality is entirely unlikely. Technically, regulatory offenses are crimes, that is, acts "committed or omitted in violation of a law forbidding or commanding it, and for which punishment is imposed upon conviction" (Morris, 1970). It is this definition criminologists should keep in mind in defining this field. Were this definition followed, the criminological conception of corporate crime would be broadened considerably (Clinard and Yeager, 1980).

3. Analyses of the origins, workings, and consequences of these economic regulatory agencies are found in a substantial body of empirical and theoretical writings by historians, political scientists, economists, and muckrakers. (For a review of this literature, see McCraw, 1975.)

4. Theories of the state, law, criminal justice, and regulation overlap and are inextricably intertwined. However, theoretical debates on the four topics are

161

conducted in their own vocabularies, with only tangential reference to parallel debates. Here we concentrate on the conjunction of state and regulatory theory. By the term *state*, we mean all the organizations that make, implement, and adjudicate laws in a given territory. Theories of the state focus on the central state. Whether our reference is to the central state or to one of the fifty states in the federal system will generally be clear from the context. When necessary, we will distinguish between the federal state and the local states.

5.   In taking this stance regarding false dichotomies, we do not wish to denigrate the importance of the many differences we are forced to ignore. We wish to provide the grounds for synthetic theory building, a project which entails considerable "vulgarization" of quite stimulating and useful intricacies.

6.   See Van Parijs (1981) for an explication of the nature and problems of functional explanations.

7.   For a discussion of the varieties of pluralism, see Nicholls (1974).

8.   Recently theoretical attention has been turned toward "corporatism," the incorporation of major interest groups within the state itself (Panitch, 1980).

9.   The valuable common component of these interpretations is the identification of real historical actors struggling to protect economic interests, demanding governmental protection from subordination to monopoly capital. The overall picture is one of class struggle involving middle classes and opposing fractions of capital. The ideological justification for railroad regulation contained three components that became the basis of further demands for regulatory reform: hostility toward monopoly power, distrust of politicians, and respect for experts. These are the basis of Progressivism, the broad social movement that often is viewed as the major source of reform and expanding governmental regulation of the economy during the first two decades of the century (McConnell, 1966). Progressivism had its roots in the various fractions of the middle class. Hostility toward monopoly emanated especially from small entrepreneurs and farmers. Trust in expertise was a reflection of the world view of the new middle class of educated employees, an emerging knowledge elite. The cleavage within the middle class has increased over time and is reflected in the "new" regulation (e.g., EPA, OSHA, OSM), which represent new middle class projects.

10.   For Mills, the power elite is comprised of three interest strata, economic, political and military elites who stand at the top of major hierarchical organizations. Mills allows for determinative weak form special interest action on all but the most basic national issues.

11. Interestingly, the strong form of special interest theory, generally viewed as conflict theory and radical critique, also has been advanced by a number of conservative theorists (e.g., Stigler, 1971).

12. The fullest exposition of this approach is found in Eric Nordlinger's monograph, *On the Autonomy of the Democratic State* (1981).

13. As indicated below, there are important exceptions (Kolko, 1965; Weinstein, 1968; Domhoff, 1970; O'Connor, 1973; Serber, 1975; Block, 1977; Kramer, 1981; Freitag, 1983; 1985).

14. Important American variants have been produced by O'Connor (1973) and Wolfe (1977). O'Connor's (1973) emphasis on the accumulation and legitimation functions (also stressed by Habermas, 1975; Offe, 1975) has been accepted widely as a summary of state functions. O'Connor (1984) subsequently addressed the state's role in the production and resolution of accumulative crises (economic downturns). Wolfe's work addressed the changing structure of the state as a response to and cause of legitimation crises.

15. The basic thrust of this idea is that the state is a steering mechanism, operating relatively independently from capitalist manipulation, but within the constraints of the capitalist system. Its major function is the rationalization of the system; that is, it is the state's task to work out emergent problems in a rapidly changing system that is subject to contradictions, crises, and disjunctions. Among the crises that must be continuously resolved are "the accumulation crisis" and the "legitimation crisis" (O'Connor, 1973). Put differently, the state must prevent economic stagnation and quell dissent. In attempting to steer the economy, the state acts as "collective capitalist," and one part of its steering function is regulation, such as controlling the supply of money, some prices and rates of profit, business competition, product quality, and economic externalities. The state acts as collective capitalist insofar as it optimizes the stability of the system, as a capitalistic system. The state need not act directly in the interests of the capitalist class in the short run. As collective capitalist, its policies necessarily damage some individual capitalists and sectors even as it aids others.

16. On the importance of class fractions or sectors in political analysis, see Freedman (1975) and Hill (1975); on social movements, see Castells (1983), Gorz (1983), and Touraine (1983).

17. It is of passing interest that class analysis of state regulation was reinvented briefly by certain pluralists to account for the emergence of social regulation in the sixties and seventies. Irving Kristol proposed that these new regulations, which were detrimental to business and economic growth, were the product of a "new class" of professional public-sector employees (1978). It is of some interest

that, for Kristol, class analysis replaces interest group analysis only when he is offended by the results of the struggle.

18. Recently McCaffrey (1982) has attempted to test the explanatory relevance of "The Capitalist State Perspective" against his data on OSHA. He finds a lack of fit, but this conclusion bears little weight since his Capitalist State theory is arbitrarily constructed from the work of quite different Marxist theorists.

19. Movement toward the development of such a model appears in several recent discussions of regulatory agencies (Bernstein, 1955; Bardach, 1977; Kagan, 1978; Mitnick, 1980; Keiser, 1980; Hawkins, 1980; Thomas, 1980; Kelman, 1980).

# 2 Surface Mining and the Environment

1. It is likely that critics are correct in designating the movement's social base as the "new class" (the "public and not-for-profit sectors" of the middle class) (Kristol, 1972; Weaver, 1978). There is some evidence that it was the professional wing of the upper-middle class, not the managerial wing, that was dominant (Devell, 1970; Cotgrove and Duff, 1981).

2. Although there has been a decline (Dunlap and Dillman, 1976), the public continues to show a high level of support for environmental concerns (Mitchell, 1980), with similar patterns across class and regional lines (Dunlap and Van Liere, 1977). Somewhat higher support for environmental activism is found among the college educated (Tognacci et al., 1972; Van Liere and Dunlap, 1980), those employed in the service sector, and those who support welfare liberalism and reject laissez faire liberalism (Honnold, 1980; Buttel and Flinn, n.d.).

# 4 The Social Construction of the Agency

1. OSM's deputy director was a federal career servant who headed the task force. Two of the five original OSM assistant directors also were federal career civil servants. The assistant director for technical services and research was a Ph.D. (engineering) and former academic who previously was employed in Pennsylvania's surface mining regulatory program. The assistant director for inspection and enforcement was an attorney. A task force volunteer, he formerly represented environmentalist and citizens' groups in litigation related to surface mining. The final assistant director position—for abandoned mined lands—was held in rapid succession by several persons.

As a group, the regional directors were knowledgeable about surface mining and several had previous experience in the regulatory area. A native of the Appalachian coal fields, the initial director in Region I was a Ph.D. in mining engineering who previously did consulting work for the mining industry. The Region II director, a native of coal producing Harlan County, Kentucky, previously had worked for the state of Kentucky in the regulatory area. Region III's director was a hydrologist and career employee of the U.S. Geological Survey. Previously he conducted research on state mining laws in the United States (Imhoff, Friz and LaFevers, 1976). The Region IV director previously worked with the U.S. Bureau of Mines and also served for two years as director of Ohio's surface mining regulatory agency. Prior to his appointment with the OSM, the Region V director served on the staff of the House of Representatives subcommittee, which was instrumental in passing the SMCRA. As a congressional staff member, he spent several years studying the problems of unregulated surface mining and the testimony of various groups involved in the legislative debates.

2. The respondent exaggerated; our data suggest that several members of the task force who "counted" initially cared more about completing their charge than about the substance of their product.

3. Historically, the problem of deficient resources has plagued regulatory agencies and accounted in part for their weak performance (Thomas, 1980). In the case of OSM, Congress wanted the agency to have sufficient resources to carry out its mandate. The task force estimated agency needs and the requisite resources were forthcoming, albeit delayed. Task force estimates proved to be generous in some areas of operation, but far short of the mark in others, such as enforcement.

The agency did face a different type of resource problem, however. No sooner had the General Services Administration put OSM into several office buildings— which complicated the process of communications—before it began to remodel the building where most of OSM was housed. It would be three years or longer before the process was completed. In the interim, employees moved offices frequently. Many times we returned to see someone after several days only to discover that the person had changed offices. The hallways of the building were cluttered with cardboard boxes and temporary files. Physical arrangements were extremely confusing.

# 5  The Social Construction of Regulations

1. Through the efforts of the environmentalists' lobby, this exact same wording was inserted into the act. It was included in the original final interim rule at their suggestion.

2. The section begins:

> Settling ponds shall be constructed in appropriate locations in each drainage area prior to any mining in that drainage area in order to control sedimentation or otherwise treat water. . . . These ponds may be used individually or in a series, and they shall meet [specified criteria].

The regulation proceeded to describe specific design standards. They consume approximately 16.75 *Federal Register* column inches.

3. Numbers were assigned to commenters by OSM administrative record office personnel. These materials are maintained in the agency's administrative record room.

4. Section 817.42 (a)(1) requires construction of sedimentation ponds.

> All surface drainage from the disturbed area, including disturbed areas that have been graded, seeded, or planted, shall be passed through a sedimentation pond, a series of ponds, or a treatment facility before leaving the permit area.

Section 817.46 contains performance and design standards for effluent control measures. It consumes 39.25 *Federal Register* column inches.

5. Based on the Universal Soil Loss Equation, *gully erosion rates,* and the appropriate *delivery ratios.*

6. Section 731.13 of the proposed permanent regulations provided:

> As part of its program submission, a State may request approval for alternatives to the requirements for permitting, bonding, inspection, enforcement and performance standards established in this Chapter where geologic, topographic, climatic, hydrologic and other regional conditions support alternative approaches. For each requirement for which the State shall—
> (a) Describe the requirement from which the variation is requested and the reason for the request;
> (b) Describe the alternative approach recommended and provide statutory or regulatory language to be used to implement the alternative; and
> (c) Explain how the alternative approach is consistent with this Chapter, including supporting data which demonstrate that use of the proposed alternative will achieve the same or more stringent regulatory results as required by this Chapter.

7. Section 731.13 of the final permanent regulations provided:

> As part of its program submission or as an amendment to an approved State program, a State may request approval for alternatives to the provisions of the regulations. . . . For each alternative provision the State shall—
> (a) Identify the provision in the regulations . . . for which the alternative is requested.
> (b) Describe the alternative proposed and provide statutory or regulatory language to be used to implement the alternatives; and

(c) Explain how and submit data, analysis and information, including identification of sources, demonstrating—

(1) that the proposed alternative will be in accordance with the applicable provisions of the Act and consistent with the regulations . . . and

(2) that the proposed alternative is necessary because of local requirements or local environmental or agricultural conditions.

8. Section 715.17 (j)(2) provides:

Surface mining and reclamation operations conducted in or adjacent to alluvial valley floors located west of the 100th meridian west longitude shall not interrupt, discontinue, or preclude farming on these valley floors.

9. Section 822.12 (c) of the final permanent regulations provides:

Surface coal mining and reclamation operations shall not cause material damage to the quality or quantity of water in surface or underground water systems that supply alluvial valley floors.

10. Section 721.13 of the proposed interim regulations provides:

(a) (1) Any person who suspects or knows of a violation of the Act, regulations or permit conditions required by the Act or of any imminent hazard may report this information in writing to the [OSM]. . . . Written complaints must be signed and include a phone number where the complaining party can be contacted. The complaint or other information shall be considered as having a reasonable basis if it alleges facts which, if proven to be true, would be sufficient to show a violation of the Act, regulations or permit. Unless the Office has reason to believe that the information is incorrect, or determines that even if true it would not constitute a violation, the Office shall conduct an inspection.

(2) The identity of any person supplying information to the Office relating to possible violations or imminent hazards shall remain confidential within the Office unless the person supplying the information consents in writing to disclosure.

(b) (1) . . . If a Federal inspection is conducted as a result of information provided to the Office, the person who provided the information shall be notified when the inspection is to occur and the person will be allowed to accompany the authorized representative during the inspection.

(2) Any person accompanying an authorized representative of the Secretary has the right of entry to, upon and through the mining and reclamation operations about which he supplied information only if he is in the presence of and is under the control, direction and supervision of the authorized representative while on the mine property.

(c) . . . Within 10 days of the inspection or, if no inspection, within 10 days of the complaint, the Office shall notify the person in writing of the following—

(1) The results of the investigation, including a description of any inspection which occurred and any enforcement action taken; copies of Federal inspection reports, notices of violation, and cessation orders may be forwarded to the person in satisfaction of this requirement;

(2) If no inspection was conducted, an explanation of the reason for not inspecting;

(3) A statement as to the person's right to informal review of the actions or inactions of the Office.

11. Section 842.12 of the final permanent regulations provides:

(a) A citizen may request a Federal inspection . . . by furnishing to an authorized representative of the Secretary a signed, written statement (or an oral report followed by a signed, written statement) giving the authorized representative reason to believe that a [violation or condition] . . . exists and setting forth a phone number and address where the citizen can be contacted.

(b) The identity of any person supplying information to the Office relating to a possible violation or imminent danger or harm shall remain confidential with the Office, if requested by that person, unless that person elects to accompany the inspector on the inspection or unless disclosure is required under the Freedom of Information Act . . . or other Federal law.

(c) If a Federal inspection is conducted . . . the citizen shall be notified as far in advance as practicable when the inspection is to occur and shall be allowed to accompany the . . . [the inspector] during the inspection. Such person has a right of entry to, upon and through the coal exploration or surface coal mining and reclamation operation . . . but only if he or she is in the presence of and is under the control, direction and supervision of . . . [the inspector] while on the mine property. Such right of entry does not include a right to enter buildings without consent of the person in control of the building or without a search warrant.

(d) Within 10 days of the Federal inspection or, if there is no inspection, within 15 days of receipt of the citizen's written statement, the Office shall send the citizen the following:

(1) If an inspection was made, a description of the enforcement action taken, which may consist of copies of the Federal inspection report and all notices of violation and cessation orders issued . . . or an explanation of why no enforcement action was taken;

(2) If no Federal inspection was conducted, an explanation of the reason why; and

(3) An explanation of the citizen's right, if any, to informal review of the action or inaction of the Office.

(e) The Office shall give copies of all materials in Paragraphs (d)(1) and (2) of this Section within the time limits specified in those paragraphs to the person alleged to be in violation, except that the name of the citizen shall be removed unless disclosure of the citizen's identity is permitted under Paragraph (b) of this Section.

# 6 The Inspection and Enforcement Program

1. The survey is described in the appendix.

2. Liberalism-conservatism was measured by a three-item scale (Cronbach's alpha = .69). Items were as follows: "One of the major tasks of government is to ensure greater economic equality among its citizens"; "one of the federal government's primary responsibilities is to direct the economy"; and "one of the major tasks of government is to ensure greater opportunity for economic equality among its citizens." Response alternatives were as follows: 4 Strongly Agree; 3 Agree; 2 Undecided; 1 Disagree; 0 Strongly Disagree. Scores on this scale ranged from a low of 0 to a high of 12. The mean score was 5.3.

3. These data are drawn from a study conducted by a group of environmentalist organizations. Results of the study were reported during the 1980 congressional oversight hearings and, more importantly, were used by plaintiffs in a suit charging the OSM with underenforcement of the act and the regulations (Council of the Southern Mountains v. Andrus, U.S. District Court, D.C., Civil Action #79–1521).

4. The Denver-based Public Lands Institute, in conjunction with faculty of the University of Denver, also examined the Region V inspection and enforcement performance for the period from May, 1978, to August, 1980. Their findings were compared to similar data collected for each of the five state regulatory programs. The results show that in 1979 OSM performed only 33 percent of the required complete inspections for the sampled mines. Inspection performance improved in the first six months of 1980, but still stood at only 58 percent. Nevertheless, OSM's performance was evaluated as superior to the I & E programs of comparable state regulatory agencies (Council of the Southern Mountains v. Andrus, 1980; Johnson et al., 1980).

5. The OSM uses a centralized penalty-assessment procedure. All assessments are made in the Washington office based on information supplied by field-level inspectors, using standard reporting forms. The following principal factors are taken into account in the assessment process: (1) the seriousness of the violation as measured by the degree of actual or potential damage it caused, and (2) the degree of operator fault represented by the violation. Using a pre-determined formula (OSM, 1980c), the assessors assign points to these (and other) categories and the points are summed. The magnitude of the assessed fine is determined by the total point score (30 CFR section 723). After the fine is assessed, the corporate offender may request a reduced fine.

6. Using records maintained by the OSM assessment office, we coded a number of variables related to the nature of the violation, the magnitude of the assessed fine, and the company's response. The major dependent variable is the magnitude of the fine assessed by the OSM for each of the NOVs. Usable data are available for 675 of the original 735 NOVs. The data were analyzed both for descriptive purposes and to examine causally the variables that affect the magnitude of assessed fines.

7. Cases were excluded where no fine was imposed, where the initial fine was vacated entirely, or where the case was still involved in the appeal process at the time of data collection.

8. Numerous investigators have examined the determinants of sentencing severity for ordinary criminal offenders (for excellent reviews see Hagan, 1974; Nettler, 1979; Kleck, 1981). This research suggests that the severity of penalties imposed on individual offenders is determined primarily by two variables: (1) the seriousness of the offense(s), and (2) the number and seriousness of previous convictions. In short, recidivists who commit "serious" offenses generally receive the most severe sentences. With rare exceptions (e.g., Lizotte, 1978), recent research shows that extra-legal characteristics of defendants have little impact on sentencing.

Although there are a number of interesting cases, studies, and exposés on the sanctioning of corporate offenders (e.g., Heilbroner et al., 1973; Geis, 1977), the issue has received little systematic research. Further, most of the available studies focus on the imposition of criminal penalties (e.g., Conklin, 1977; Goff and Reasons, 1978; Snider, 1982). Clinard and Yeager's study of the illegal behaviors of 582 American corporations is an important exception to this pattern of neglect.

9. Assessed negligence was operationalized as the number of points OSM's assessors awarded based on their appraisal of the relative importance of negligence versus willfulness manifested in the offender's violation. An increasing number of points (up to thirty) are awarded according to whether the violation suggested (1) no negligence, (2) negligence, (3) recklessness, or (4) knowing and willful misconduct (OSM, 1980c:26).

10. Assessed damage was operationalized as the total number of points OSM's assessors awarded for the actual or potential damage to property, individuals, or the environment caused by the violative activity. Assessors can impose a maximum of thirty points for damage (OSM, 1980c:17–24). The least serious violations are those for which the assessor, on the basis of the inspection report, believes there was little actual or potential damage. By the same token, the most serious violations are those for which the degree of real or potential damage is adjudged to be high.

11. The damage points assessed by the OSM emphasize the relative seriousness of a particular type of violation. By contrast, the concept of seriousness in the criminological literature generally refers to the relative heinousness of different kinds of violations, measured by the maximum sentence allowed by statute (e.g., Hagen et al., 1980) or by ranking of offenses by the public (e.g., Sellin and Wolfgang, 1964; Rossi et al., 1974). To test a similar concept of seriousness, we constructed our own seriousness index (compare Clinard and Yeager, 1980). In doing so, we used the available literature of groups opposed to surface coal mining as well as the interviews we conducted with OSM personnel and

environmentalists. These sources enabled us to rank order sanctionable mining practices according to their immediate or potential harm to private property, public health, or the environment. Three points were assigned to the most serious violations (e.g., placement of spoil on the downslope, altering the chemical balance or siltation level of existing water sources), two points to moderately serious violations (e.g., improper revegetation practices, insufficient segregation of removed topsoil), and one point to the least serious violations (e.g., failure to post adequate signs or markers on the mine site, failure to maintain proper records of mining activities).

12. Size of mining corporation was operationalized as coal tonnage produced during the year 1979 (National Coal Association, 1980). We grouped this variable into three categories. Small companies are those that produced less than 300,000 tons of coal during 1979; medium-sized companies produced between 300,000 and 1,000,000 tons of coal; and large companies produced over 1,000,000 tons of coal.

13. Hagen et al. (1979) describe the criminal justice system as a "loosely coupled system." In such a system, seriousness of offenses may be independent of sanction severity. In contrast, the OSM used an assessment system that tightly conjoined their evaluation of offense seriousness and the amount of the fine.

14. In their efforts to create an I & E program that was non-discretionary and contained penalties severe enough to serve as a deterrent, members of the I & E task group scrutinized the enforcement programs of other regulatory agencies for clues as to what might be useful, and avoidable, for the OSM. One aspect of the OSM program was constructed to avoid a problem the Mine Safety and Health Administration (MSHA) had encountered: difficulties in collecting civil penalties. Unlike MSHA, the OSM program requires cited coal operators to pay their fines *before* they can appeal their violations. These funds are held in escrow until final disposition of the appeal, after which they are returned to the operator if the agency's action is reversed.

15. The collection of fines involves several steps within the federal bureaucracy. Once assessed, the violator has a period of time (thirty to ninety days) to appeal the penalty in a regional conference. These conferences usually produce a 50 percent reduction in the initial fine imposed by the Assessment Office. Following expiration of the appeal period, the OSM initiates collection efforts. If unsuccessful, the fine is referred to a contractor who reviews the file, determines the final assessment, and tries to collect the fine. If full payment is not forthcoming, the case may be referred to the Department of Justice.

# 7 Regional Variation in Inspection and Enforcement

1. Due to regional inconsistencies in record keeping during the early months, we chose a twelve-month period from July 1, 1979, through June 30, 1980, to examine OSM's inspection and enforcement performance in the two regions. This period avoided the impact of funding and staffing delays that occurred in the early enforcement period. Also, by late 1980 many of the western states had acquired primacy, and OSM's enforcement activities were curtailed sharply in Region West.

2. Reliable statistics for earlier years are not available.

3. Use of such a base measure can be defended as a surrogate measure of the total volume of earth that must be moved in mining operations. In turn, this serves as a reasonable measure of the total volume of mining activity that is potentially sanctionable.

4. See appendix for more detail about research methodology.

5. Due to the low number of respondents in Region West, the statistics must be interpreted with caution.

6. Technically, we note that the three items that constitute the conciliatory scale focus on *educating* mine operators; there are not items dealing with a variety of *negotiational* enforcement strategies.

7. In 1979, eighteen of the nation's largest coal producing surface mines were located in Region West. None were located in Region East (National Coal Association, 1980).

8. OSM's centralized office for assessing civil penalties was a special irritant to Region East personnel. They preferred a decentralized assessment process so that the regions would set penalties. Presumably such a procedure would have permitted them to tailor penalties flexibly and thus reward operators who were making a good faith effort to comply with the regulations.

# 8 The Agency Under Siege

1. As originally introduced, S.1403 would have granted the states a seven-month extension of the deadline for submission of primacy applications.

2. The national media noted these efforts. The *Washington Post* proclaimed editorially that Congress should not "strip the mining act" (20 August 1980).

3. Actually, the ad lodged several complaints about coal mining regulation that went far beyond OSM to federal policies generally.

4. The flavor of his testimony can be gained from an excerpt:

> As [OSM's] regulations were being drafted, the senior level staff of OSM, myself included, had numerous meetings to review and revise the proposed language. It became obvious to me early in the review process that the direction being taken by the agency was to make the regulations punitive, to remove from the States as much flexibility as possible, to straitjacket the operators with design criteria, [and] to write regulations on every conceivable issue. [U.S. Congress, House, 1980:83–84]

He also charged that "OSM seemed to pay attention mostly to the more strident environmentalists" and that "it appeared that satisfying [them] was more important than satisfying the law" (U.S. Congress, House, 1980:82–83).

5. Descriptions provided by insiders are supported by media accounts of the outcome of the OSM-CEA meeting. The *New York Times* said that the CEA's

> tardy intervention—relying heavily, as it turned out, on the coal industry's own data—further delayed the timetable . . . [b]ut in the end it appears to have had little impact on the regulations. [Franklin, 1979]

6. It was during this time that regional personnel began referring to headquarters as "the Bunker."

7. The Department's deputy assistant secretary for energy and minerals, whom the coal industry viewed as a regulatory hard-liner, was dismissed at the same time.

# 9 A Theoretical Reprise

1. The National Research Council (1981b:200) has summarized the incremental reclamation costs produced by Public Law 95–87 for a typical mine in each of the three U.S. coal fields. The estimated costs (in 1978 dollars) were $5.24 per ton in Appalachia, $1.80 per ton in the Midwest, and $0.57 per ton in the West. The major sources of these differences are spoil handling costs.

2. For economists the major options in regulatory control are regulation by economic incentive versus regulation by administrative direction (Mitnick, 1980: ch.6). Although the incentive option, a favorite scheme of academic economists,

has been proposed for surface mining (National Research Council, 1981), it never has been considered seriously as a feasible political alternative in this area. Thus, the options that must be addressed in the regulation of surface mining are variants of the directive approach.

3.  Opponents of the OSM often charged that it was guided by an "environmentalist" ideology. We regard environmentalism as a subtype of the broader "reformist" ideology.

4.  The values, ideology, and politics of the "new class" are discussed in Gouldner (1979), Walker (1979), Bruce-Biggs (1979), Stabile (1984), and Oppenheimer (1985).

# Coda    The Office of Surface Mining Since 1980

1.  The original state window read as follows:

> (a) With regard to the Act, the state laws and regulations are no less stringent than, meet the minimum requirements of and include all applicable provisions of the Act.
> (b) With regard to the Secretary's regulations, the state laws and regulations are no less stringent than and meet the applicable provisions of the regulations of this chapter. [section 730.5(a), (b)]

The major substantive change in the new state window was made in section 730.5(b) to read as follows:

> With regard to the Secretary's regulations, the state laws and regulations are no less effective than the Secretary's regulations in meeting the requirements of the Act.

2.  It is unlikely that Reagan's often-stated opposition to regulations had any important bearing on his election. It was not a key issue in the campaign and public opinion polls show no decline in support for environmental regulation (Mitchell, 1984).

3.  This instrumentalist action was, of course, not a form of corporate liberalism. It was a reactionary revision of reform rather than a cooptation of reform.

# Bibliography

Ackerman, B.A., and Hassler, W.T.
  1981   *Clean Coal/Dirty Air.* New Haven, Conn.: Yale University Press.
Althusser, Louis
  1970   *Reading Capital.* London: New Left Books.
Appalachian Land Ownership Task Force
  1983   *Who Owns Appalachia? Land Ownership and Its Impact.* Lexington: University Press of Kentucky.
Arrow, Kenneth J.
  1981   "Regulation." *Federation of American Scientists Public Interest Report* 34(June):11–12.
Bardach, Eugene
  1977   *The Implementation Game.* Cambridge, Mass.: MIT Press.
Bardach, Eugene and Robert A. Kagan
  1982   *Going by the Book: Unreasonableness in Protective Regulation.* Philadelphia: Temple University Press.
Benson, Lee
  1955   *Merchants, Farmers and Railroads: Rail Regulation and New York Politics, 1850–1887.* Cambridge, Mass.: Harvard University Press.
Berman, Daniel
  1978   *Death on the Job: Occupational Health and Safety Struggles in the United States.* Monthly Review Press.
Bernstein, Marver H.

1955    *Regulating Business by Independent Commission.* Princeton, N.J.: Princeton University Press.

Block, Fred
1977    "The ruling class does not rule." *Socialist Revolution* 33(MAy):6–28.
1981    "Beyond relative autonomy: State managers as historical subjects." *New Political Science* 2(Fall):33–49.

Bowles, Samuel, and Gintis, Herbert
1982    "The crisis of liberal democratic capitalism: The case of the United States." *Politics and Society* 11(1):51–93.

Braithwaite, John
1985    *To Punish or Persuade: Enforcement of Coal Mine Safety.* Albany: State University of New York Press.

Bruce-Biggs, B., ed.
1979    *The New Class?* New Brunswick, N.J.: Transaction Books.

Buck, Solon Justis
1913    *The Granger Movement.* Cambridge, Mass.: Harvard University Press.

Burns, T., and Stalker, G. DM.
1961    *The Management of Innovation.* London: Tavistock.

Buttel, Frederick W., and Flinn, William L.
n.d.    "Politics and the environment: The relationship among political attitudes, employment sector, and environmental concern." (Unpublished paper).

Calavita, Kitty
1983    "The demise of the occupational safety and health administration: A case study in symbolic policies." *Social Problems* 30(April):437–48.

Carnoy, Martin
1984    *The State and Theory.* Princeton: Princeton University Press.

Carter, R.P., et al.
1974    *Surface Mined Land in the Midwest.* Argonne, Ill.: Argonne National Laboratory.

Castells, Manuel
1980    *The Economic Crisis and American Society.* Princeton: Princeton University Press.
1983    *The City and the Grassroots: A Cross-Cultural Theory of Urban Social Movements.* Berkeley: University of California Press.

Caudill, Marry M.
1963    *Night Comes to the Cumberlands.* Boston: Little, Brown & Co.

1971   *My Land is Dying.* New York: Dutton.
Center for Law and Social Policy and Environmental Policy Institute
1978   *The Strip Mine Handbook.* Washington, D.C.: Brophy Associates, Inc.
Chilton, Kenneth
1979   *A Decade of Rapid Growth in Federal Regulation.* St. Louis: Center for the Study of American Business, Washington University.
Clark, Terry
1967   "The concept of power." *Social Science Quarterly* 48(December):271–86.
Clinard, Marshall B., and Yeager, Peter C.
1980   *Corporate Crime.* New York: The Free Press.
*Coal Age*
1976   "Carter blocks out his coal policies." *Coal Age* 81(December):21–23.
*Coal Facts*
1976   Washington, D.C.: National Coal Association.
Conklin, John E.
1977   *Illegal But Not Criminal.* Englewood Cliffs, N.J.: Prentice-Hall.
Cotgrove, Stephen, and Duff, Andrew
1981   "Environmentalism, values, and social change." *British Journal of Sociology* 32(March):92–110.
Council of the Southern Mountains, Inc. et al. vs. Andrus
1979   Memorandum Opinion and Order of the U.S. District Court for the District of Columbia (Civil Action No. 79–1521).
Dahl, Robert A.
1967   *Pluralist in the United States: Conflict and Consent.* Chicago: Rand McNally & Co.
Dale, Lawrence B.
1978   "The Surface Mining Control and Reclamation Act of 1977." *St. Mary's Law Journal* 9:863–92.
Devall, William B.
1970   "Conservation: An upper-middle class social movement: A replication." *Journal of Leisure Research* 2:123–26.
Domhoff, G. William
1970   *The Higher Circles: The Governing Class in America.* New York: Random House.
1978   *The Powers That Be: Processes of Ruling Class Domination in America.* New York: Random House.
1983   *Who Rules America Now?* Englewood Cliffs, N.J.: Prentice-Hall.

Donnelly, Patrick G.
1982 "The origins of the Occupational Safety and Health Act of 1970." *Social Problems* 30(October):13–25.

Downs, Anthony
1967 *Inside Bureaucracy.* Boston: Little, Brown & Co.

Dunlap, Riley E., and Dillman, Don A.
1976 "Decline in support for environmental protection: Evidence from a 1970–1974 panel study." *Rural Sociology* 41(Fall):382–90.

Dunlap, Riley E., and Van Liere Kent D.
1977 "Declining public support for environmental protection: 'Ecological backlash' or 'natural decline'." Paper presented at the annual meetings of the Rural Sociological Society, Madison, Wisconsin.

Eichbaum, William M., and Babcock, Hope M.
1982 "A question of delegation: The Surface Mining Control and Reclamation Act of 1977 and state-federal relations. An inquiry into the success with which Congress may provide detailed guidance for executive agency action." *Dickinson Law Review* 86(Summer):615–46.

*Energy Daily*
1978 "Surface mining law takes on a regional flavor." August 1.

Environmental Policy Center
1982 *The Federal Strip Mine Law Five Years Later.* Background Assessment, Washington, D.C.: Environmental Policy Center, Zerox.

Erickson, Kai T.
1976 *Everything in its Path.* New York: Simon and Schuster.

Erskine, Hazel
1972 "The polls: Pollution and its costs." *Public Opinion Quarterly* 36(Spring):120–35.

Faich, Ronald, and Gale, Richard
1971 "The environmental movement: From recreation to politics." *Pacific Sociological Review* 14:270–87.

Fisher, Steve, and Foster, Jim
1979 "Models for furthering revolutionary praxis in Appalachia." *Appalachian Journal* 6(Spring):171–96.

Frand, Nancy
1983 "From criminal to civil penalties in the history of health and safety laws." *Social Problems* 30(June):532–44.

Franklin, Ben A.
1979 "A blueprint against doing violence to the land." *New York Times,* March 11.

Freedman, Francesca
1975    "The internal structure of the American proletariat." *Socialist Revolution* 5(October):41–83.
Freitag, Peter J.
1983    "The myth of corporate capture: Regulatory commissions in the United States." *Social Problems* 30(April):480–91.
1985    "Class conflict and the rise of government regulation." *Insurgent Sociologist* 12(Winter):51–66.
Friendly, Henry J.
1962    *The Federal Administrative Agencies: The Need for a Better Definition of Standards.* Cambridge, Mass.: Harvard University Press.
Galbraith, John K.
1952    *American Capitalism: The Concept of Countervailing Power.* Boston: Houghton Mifflin Co.
Gardiner, John A.
1969    *Traffic and the Police.* Cambridge, Mass.: Harvard University Press.
Geis, Gilbert
1977    "The heavy electrical equipment antitrust cases of 1961." Pp. 117–32 in Gilbert Geis and Robert F. Meier, eds. *White-Collar Crime.* rev. ed. New York: The Free Press.
Gersuny, Carl
1981    *Work Hazards and Industrial Conflict.* Hanover: University Press of New England.
Goff, Colin H., and Reasons, Charles E.
1978    *Corporate Crime in Canada.* Englewood Cliffs, N.J.: Prentice-Hall.
Gold, David A., Lo, Clarence Y.H., and Wright, Erik Olin
1975    "Recent developments in Marxist theories of the capitalist state." *Monthly Review* 27(October and November):29–43, 36–51.
Gorz, Andre
1982    *Farewell to the Working Class.* Boston: South End Press.
Gouldner, Alvin
1979    *The Future of Intellectuals and the Rise of the New Class.* New York: Seabury.
Grimm, Elmore C., and Hill, Ronald D.
1974    *Environmental Protection in Surface Mining of Coal.* Cincinnati: Environmental Protection Agency.
Habermas, Jurgen
1975    *Legitimation Crisis.* Boston: Beacon.

Hagan, John
1974 "Extra-legal attributes and criminal sentencing: An assessment of a sociological viewpoint." *Law and Society Review* 8(Spring):357–84.
Hagan, John, Hewitt, J.D., and Alwin, D.F.
1979 "Ceremonial justice: Crime and punishment in a loosely coupled system." *Social Forces* 58(December):506–27.
Hagan, John, Nagle, I., and Albonetti, C.
1980 "The differential sentencing of white-collar offenders in ten federal district courts." *American Sociological Review* 45(October):802–20.
Handler, Joel F.
1978 *Social Movements and the Legal System.* New York: Academic Press.
Hardin, Garrett
1968 "The tragedy of the commons." *Science* 162(13 December):1243–48.
Harry, Joseph P.
1974 "Causes of contemporary environmentalism." *Humboldt Journal of Social Relations* 2:1–7.
Harry, Joseph P., Gale, Richrd P., and Hendee, John C.
1969 "Conservation: An upper-middle class social movement." *Journal of Leisure Research* 3:129–31.
Harvey, D. Michael
1978 "Paradise regained? Surface Mining Control and Reclamation Act of 1977." *Houston Law Review* 15:1147–74.
Hawkins, Keith
1980 "The use of discretion by regulatory officials: A case study of environmental pollution in the United Kingdom." Draft paper presented to Baldy Center for Law and Social Policy, Conference on Law, Discretion and Bureaucratic Behavior (June).
1984 *Environment and Enforcement: Regulation and the Social Definition of Pollution.* New York: Oxford.
Heilbroner, R.L., et al., eds.
1973 *In the Name of Profit.* New York: Warner Paperback Library.
Heatherly, Charles L., ed.
1981 *Mandate for Leadership.* Washington, D.C.: The Heritage Foundation.
Hill, Judah
1975 *Class Analysis: The United States in the 1970s.* Emeryville: Class Analysis.
Hirsch, Joachim

1978 "The state apparatus and social reproduction: Elements of a theory of the bourgeois state," in John Holloway and Sol Picciotto, eds. *State and Capital: A Marxist Debate.* London: Arnold.

Hodel vs. Virginia Surface Mining and Reclamation Association
1980 Memorandum opinion and order of the U.S. District Court for the District of Columbia.

Honnold, Julia
1980 "Changes in predictors of public concern in the 1970s." Paper presented at the annual meetings of the Society for the Study of Social Problems, New york.

Humphrey, Craig R., and Buttel, Frederick R.
1982 *Environment, Energy and Society.* Belmont, Calif.: Wadsworth.

Hunter, Floyd
1959 *Top Leadership, U.S.A.* Chapel Hill: University of North Carolina Press.

Imhoff, E.A., Friz, T.O., and LaFevers, J.R.
1976 *A Guide to State Programs for the Reclamation of Surface Mined Lands.* Washington, D.C.: U.S. Geological Survey (Circular #731).

Interstate Mining Compact Commission
n.d. Untitled. Lexington, KY: Interstate Mining Compact Commission.
1978 *Annual Report—1978.* Lexintgon, KY: Interstate Mining Compact Commission.
1979 *Annual Report—1979.* Lexington, KY: Interstate Mining Compact Commission.
1981 *Annual Report—1981.* Lexington, KY: Interstate Mining Compact Commission.

Jessop, Bob
1982 *The Capitalist State.* New York: New York University Press.

Johnson, C.R., May, D.S., and Pring, G.W.
1980 *Stripping the Law on Coal.* Denver: Public Lands Institute.

Kagan, Robert A.
1978 *Regulatory Justice.* New York: Russell Sage Foundation.
1980 "The positive uses of discretion: The good inspector." Paper presented to the Law and Society Association, Madison, Wisconsin, (June).

Kagan, Robert A., and Scholz, John T.
1984 "The 'criminology of the corporation' and regulatory enforcement strategies." In Keith Hawkins and John M. Thomas, eds.

*Enforcing Regulation: Policy and Practice.* Boston: Kluwer Nijhoff.

Keiser, K. Robert
1980 "The new regulation of Health and Safety." *Political Science Quarterly* 95(Fall):479–91.

Kelman, Steven:
1974 "Regulation by the numbers—A report on the Consumer Product Safety Commission." *The Public Interest* 36(Summer):83–102.
1980 "Occupational Safety and Health Administration." Pp. 236–66 in James Q. Wilson, ed. *The Politics of Regulation.* New York: Basic Books.
1981 *Regulating America, Regulating Sweden,* Cambridge, Mass.: MIT Press.

Klaas, Michael W., and Weiss, Leonard W.
1978 *Framework for Regulation.* Washington, D.C.: The Brookings Institution.

Kleck, Gary
1981 "Racial discrimination in criminal sentencing." *American Sociological Review* 46(December):783–805.

Kolko, Gabriel
1963 *The Triumph of Conservatism: A Reinterpretation of American History, 1900–1916.* New York: The Free Press.
1965 *Railroads and Regulation: 1877–1916.* New York: W.W. Norton.

Kramer, Ronald C.
1981 "On the social origins of federal regulatory law." Paper presented at the Annual Meeting of the American Society of Criminology, Washington, D.C.

Kristol, Irving
1972 "About equality." *Commentary* (November).
1978 *Two Cheers for Capitalism.* New York: Basic Books.

Landy, Marc Karnis
1976 *The Politics of Environmental Reform: Controlling Kentucky Strip Mining.* Washington, D.C.: Resources for the Future.

Lasswell, Harold D.
1935 *Politics: Who Gets what, when, how.* New York: McGraw-Hill.

Lilly, William, III, and Miller III, James C.
1977 "The new 'social regulation'." *The Public Interest* 47(Spring):49–61.

Lizotte, Alan J.

1978    "Extra-legal factors in Chicago's criminal justice courts." *Social Problems* 25(June):564–80.

Lowi, Theodore
1969    *The End of Liberalism.* New York: W.W. Norton.

Lynxwiler, John P., and Groce, Stephen B.
1981    "Violative behavior and the negotiation of public identities in the work setting: An analysis of Appalachian mine operators." Paper presented at the annual meeting of the Southern Sociological Society, Louisville, Kentucky (April 9).

McCaffrey, David P.
1982    *OSHA and the Politics of Health Regulation.* New York: Plenum.

McCarthy, John D., and Zald, Mayer N.
1973    *The Trends of Social Movements in America: Professionalization and Resource Mobilization.* Morristown, N.J.: General Learning Press.

McConnell, Grant
1966    *Private Power and American Democracy.* New York: Knopf.

McCraw, Thomas K.
1975    "Regulation in America: A review article." *Business History Review* 49(Summer):159–83.

Manning, Peter K.
1977    *Police Work.* Cambridge, Mass.: MIT Press.
1980    *The Narcs' Game.* Cambridge, Mass.: MIT Press.

Mansfield, Edward
1980    "Federal Maritime Commission." Pp. 42–74 in James Q. Wilson, ed. *The Politics of Regulation.* New York: Basic Books.

Marcus, Alfred
1980    "Environmental Protection Agency." Pp. 267–303 in James Q. Wilson, ed. *The Politics of Regulation.* New York: Basic Books.

Martin, Albro
1971    *Enterprise Denied: Origins of the Decline of American Railroads, 1897–1917.* New York: Columbia University Press.

Mendeloff, John
1979    *Regulating Safety: An Economic and Political Analysis of Occupational Safety and Health Policy.* Cambridge, Mass.: MIT Press.

Menzel, Donald C.
1981    "Implementation of the Federal Surface Mining Control and Reclamation Act of 1977." *Public Administration Review* 41(Summer).

Michels, Robert

1962 *Political Parties.* New York: Free Press.
Miliband, Ralph
1969 *The State in Capitalist Society.* New York: Basic Books.
Miller, George H.
1971 *Railroads and the Granger Laws.* Madison: University of Wisconsin.
Mills, C. Wright
1956 *The Power Elite.* New York: Oxford University Press.
Mitchell, Robert Cameron
1979 "National environmental lobbies and the apparent illogic of collective action." PP. 87–121 in Clifford S. Russell, ed. *Collective Decision Making.* Baltimore: The John Hopkins University Press.
1980 *Public Opinion on Environmental Issues.* Washington, D.C.: U.S. Government Printing Office.
Mitnick, Barry M.
1980 *The Political Economy of Regulation.* New York: Columbia University Press.
Mosley, Hugh
1982 "Capital and the state: West German neo-orthodox state theory." *Review of Radical Political Economics* 14(Spring):24–32.
*Mountain Life and Work*
1980 "Inspectors trap strip mine wildcatters in helicopter raid." *Mountain Life and Work* 56(June):37–8.
Munn, Robert F.
1975 "The development of strip mining in southern Appalachia." *Appalachian Journal* 3(Autumn):87–93.
Nash, Gerald D.
1957 "Origins of the Interstate Commerce Act of 1887." *Pennsylvania History* 24:181–90.
National Coal Association
1980 *Keystone Coal Industry Manual.* New York: McGraw-Hill.
National Research Council
1977 *Decision Making in the Environmental Protection Agency.* Washington, D.C.: National Academy of Sciences.
1981 *Coal Mining and Ground-Water Resources in the United States.* Washington, D.C.: National Academy Press.
1981a *Disposal of Excess Spoil from Coal Mining and the Surface Mining Control and Reclamation Act of 1977.* Washington, D.C.: National Academy Press.
1981b *Surface Mining: Soil, Coal, and Society.* Washington, D.C.: National Academy Press.

Nettler, Gwynn
1979   "Criminal Justice." *Annual Review of Sociology* 5:27-52.
Nicholls, David
1974   *Three Varieties of Pluralism.* New York: St. Martin's Press.
Nivola, Pietro S.
1978   "Distributing a municipal service: A case study of housing inspection." *Journal of Politics* 40:59-81.
Nordlinger, Eric
1981   *On the Autonomy of the Democratic State.* Cambridge, Mass.: Harvard University Press.
O'Conner, James
1973   *The Fiscal Crisis of the State.* New York: St. Martin's Press.
1984   *Accumulation Crisis.* New York: Blackwell.
Offe, Claus
1974   "Structural problems of the capitalist state." In Klaus von Beyme, ed. *German Political Studies.* Beverly Hills, Calif.: Sage Publications.
1975   "The theory of the capitalist state and the problem of policy formation." Pp. 125-44 in Leon Lindberg, Robert Alford, Colin Crouch, and Claus Offe, eds. *Stress and Contradiction in Modern Capitalism.* Lexington: Lexington Books.
Office of Surface Mining Reclamation and Enforcement
1980c   *Penalty Assessment Manual.* Washington, D.C.: Branch of Assessment, Division of Enforcement.
1980d   *Regional Memo*—Field Office.
1981   *Inspectable Units.* January 6.
1981a   *Office of Surface Mining Reorganization.* June 12.
1981e   *Schedule for Regulatory Reform.* n.d.
Oppenheimer, Martin
1985   *White Collar Politics.* New York: Monthly Review Press.
Owen, Bruce M., and Braeutigam, Ronald
1978   *The Regulation Game.* Cambridge, Mass.: Ballinger.
Panitch, Leo
1980   "Recent theorizations of corporatism: Reflections on a growth industry." *British Journal of Sociology* 31(June):159-87.
Parsons, Talcott
1967   *Sociological Theory and Modern Society.* New York: Free Press.
Poulantzas, Nicos
1969   "The problem of the capitalist state." *New Left Review* 58(November):67-78.
1973   *Political Power and Social Classes.* London: New Left Books.
1978   *State, Power, and Socialism.* London: New Left Books.

President's Commission on Coal
  1980  *Coal Data Book.* Washington, D.C.: U.S. Government Printing Office.
Quirk, Paul J.
  1980  "Food and Drug Administration." Pp. 191–235 in James Q. Wilson, ed. *The Politics of Regulation.* New York: Basic Books.
  1981  *Industry Influence in Federal Regulatory Agencies.* Princeton, N.J.: Princeton University Press.
Reiger, John F.
  1975  *American Sportsmen and the Origins of Conservation.* New York: Winchester.
Reiss, Albert J., Jr., and Bordua, David J.
  1966  "Environment and organization: A perspective on the police." Pp. 25–55 in David J. Bordua, ed. *The Police: Six Sociological Essays.* New York: John Wiley & Sons.
Rossi, P.H., Waite, E., Bose, C.E., and Berk, R.E.
  1974  "The seriousness of crimes: Normative structure and individual differences." *American Sociological Review* 39(April):224–37.
Rowland, C.K., and Marz, Roger
  1982  "Gresham's Law: The regulatory analogy." *Policy Studies Review* 1:572–80.
  1975  "Social movements and regulatory agencies: Toward a more adequate—and less pessimistic—theory of 'clientele capture'." *Policy Sciences* 6(September):301–42.
Sabatier, Paul A., and Mazmanian, Daniel A.
  1983  *Can Regulation Work? The Implementation of the 1972 California Coastline Initiative.* New York: Plenum.
Salamon, L.B., and Wamsley, G.L.
  1976  "The federal bureaucracy: Responsible to whom?" Pp. 151–88 in L.M. Reichenbach, ed. *The Responsiveness of American institutions.* Bloomington: Indiana University Press.
Save Our Cumberland Mountains
  1978  *A Study of Tennessee Strip Mine Enforcement, 1972–77.* East Tennessee Research Corporation.
  1981  *A Study of Tennessee Strip Mine Enforcement.* East Tennessee Research Corporation.
Schneider, David A.
  1971  "Strip mining in Kentucky." *Kentucky Law Journal* 59:652–72.
Sellin, Thorsten, and Wolfgang, Marvin
  1964  *Measurement of Delinquency.* New York: John Wiley & Sons.
Serber, David

1975 "Regulating reform: The social organization of insurance regulation." *The Insurgent Sociologist* 3(Spring):83-105.

Sharfman, I.L.
1931 *The Interstate Commerce Commission*, vol. 1. New York: Commonwealth Fund.

Shapiro, Susan P.
1980 *Thinking About White-Collar Crime.* Washington, D.C.: U.S. Department of Justice, National Institute of Justice.

Snider, Laureen
1982 "Traditional and corporate theft: A comparison of sanctions." Pp. 235-58 in Peter Wickman and Timothy Dailey, eds. *White-Collar and Economic Crime.* Lexington, Mass.: D.C. Heath.

Stabile, Donald
1984 *Prophets of Order.* Boston: South End Press.

Stigler, George J.
1971 "The theory of economic regulations." *Bell Journal of Economics and Management Science* 2(Spring):3-21.

Thomas, John M.
1980 "The regulatory role in the containment of corporate illegality." Pp. 107-40 in Herbert Edelhertz, ed., *The Development of a Research Agenda on White-Collar Crime.* Seattle: Battelle Human Affairs Research Centers.

Tognacci, Louis, R., Weigel, R.A., Wideen, M.F., and Vernon, D.
1971 "Environmental quality—how universal is public concern? *Environment and Behavior* 4:73-86.

Touraine, Alain
1981 *The Voice and the Eye: An Analysis of Social Movements.* New York: Cambridge University Press.

U.S. Congress, House of Representatives
1972 *Regulation of Strip Mining.* Hearings before the Subcommittee on Mines and Mining of the Committee on Interior and Insular Affairs. 92nd Cong., 1st sess. Washington, D.C.: U.S. Government Printing Office.

1973 *Regulation of Surface Mining.* Hearings before the Subcommittee on Environment and the Subcommiteee on Mines and Mining of the Committee on Interior and Insular Affairs. 93rd Cong., 1st sess. Washington, D.C.: U.S. Government Printing Office.

1975 *Veto of the Surface Mining Control and Reclamation Act of 1975.* 94th Cong., 1st sess. Washington, D.C.: U.S. Government Printing Office.

1977    *Surface Mining Control and Reclamation Act of 1977.* Hearings before the Subcommittee on Energy and the Environment of the Committee on Interior and Insular Affairs. 95th Cong., 1st sess. Washington, D.C.: U.S. Government Printing Office.

1977a   *Surface Mining Control and Reclamation Act of 1977.* Report of the Committee on Interior and Insular Affairs. 95th Cong., 1st sess. Washington, D.C.: U.S. Government Printing Office.

1978    *Implementation of the Surface Mining Control and Reclamation Act of 1977.* Oversight Hearings before the Subcommittee on Energy and the Environment of the Committee on Interior and Insular Affairs. 95th Cong., 2nd sess. Washington, D.C.: U.S. Government Printing Office.

1979    *Implementation of the Surface Mining Control and Reclamation Act of 1977.* Oversight Hearings before Subcommittee on Energy and the Environment of the Committee on Interior and Insular Affairs. 96th Cong., 1st sess. Washington, D.C.: U.S. Government Printing Office.

1980    *Oversight on the Surface Mining Control and Reclamation Act of 1977.* Oversight Hearings before the Subcommittee on Energy and the Environment of the Committee on Interior and Insular Affairs. 96th Cong., 2nd sess. Washington, D.C.: U.S. Government Printing Office.

1981    *Implementation of the Surface Mining Control and Reclamation Act of 1977.* Oversight Hearings before Subcommittee on Energy and Environment of the Committee on Interior and Insular Affairs. 97th Cong., 1st sess. Washington, D.C.: U.S. Government Printing Office.

1981a   *Reorganization of the Office of Surface Mining.* Oversight Hearings before Subcommittee on Energy and the Environment of the Committee on Interior and Insular Affairs. 97th Cong., 1st sess. Washington, D.C.: U.S. Government Printing Office.

1982    *Oversight Hearing on the Office of Surface Mining Reclamation and Enforcement Budget for Fiscal Year 1983.* Subcommittee on Energy and the Environment of the Committee on Interior and Insular Affairs. Xerox.

U.S. Congress, Senate
1968    *Surface Mining Reclamation.* Hearings before the Committee on Interior and Insular Affairs. 90th Cong., 2nd sess. Washington, D.C.: U.S. Government Printing Office.

1972    *Surface Mining.* Hearings before the subcommittee on Minerals, Materials, and Fuels of the Committee on Interior and Insular

Affairs. 92nd Cong., 1st sess. Washington, D.C.: U.S. Government Printing Office.

1979 *Oversight—The Surface Mining Control and Reclamation Act of 1977.* Hearings before the Committee on Energy and Natural Resources. 96th Cong., 1st sess. Washington, D.C.: U.S. Government Printing Office.

1981 *Harris, Stearns, and Richards Nominations.* Hearing before the Committee on Energy and Natural Resources. 97th Cong. 1st sess. Washington, D.C.: U.S. Government Printing Office.

U.S. Department of Energy

1980 *Coal Data: A Reference.* Washington, D.C.: Energy Information Administration.

1981 *Coal Production—1979.* Washington, D.C.: Energy Information Administration.

1982 *1981 Annual Report to Congress. Volume 2, Energy Statistics.* Washington, D.C.: Energy Information Administration, May.

U.S. Department of the Interior

1967 *Surface Mining and Our Environment.* Washington, D.C.: U.S. Government Printing Office.

U.S. Department of Justice

1982 *Letter to the Surface Mining Project, University of Tennessee, May 6.*

*U.S. Department of Labor*

*1981 Technology, Productivity, and Labor in the Bituminous Coal Industry, 1950–1979.* Washington, D.C.: U.S. Government Printing Office.

Van Liere, Kent D., and Dunlap, Riley

1980 "The social bases for environmental concern." *Public Opinion Quarterly* 44(Spring):181–97.

Van Parijs, Philippe

1981 *Evolutionary Explanation in the Social Sciences.* New York: Tavistock.

Walker, Pat, ed.

1979 *Between Labor and Capital.* Boston: South End Press.

Wallerstein, Immanuel

1979 *The Capitalist World Economy.* New York: Cambridge University Press.

Weaver, Paul H.

1978 "Regulation, social policy, and class conflict." *The Public Interest* 50(Winter):45–63.

Weber, Max

1978 *Economy and Society.* Berkeley: University of California Press.

Weinstein, James
  1968   *The Corporate Ideal in the Liberal State: 1900–1918.* Boston:
          Beacon.
Wiener, Daniel P.
  1980   *Reclaiming the West: The Coal Industry and Surface Mined
          Lands.* New York: Inform, Inc.
Wilson, James Q.
  1968   *Varieties of Police Behavior.* Cambridge, Mass.: Harvard Uni-
          versity Press.
  1978   *The Investigators.* New York: Basic Books.
  1980   *The Politics of Regulation.* New York: Basic Books.
Wolfe, Alan
  1977   *The Limits of Legitimacy.* New York: Free Press.
Ziegler, L.H., and Peak, G.W.
  1972   *Interest Groups in American Society.* 2d ed. Englewood Cliffs,
          N.J.: Prentice-Hall.

# Index

191